LINKEDWORKING

Generating Success On
The World's Largest
Professional Networking Website

Frank Agin and Lewis Howes

www.linkedworking.com

Advanced Praise For
LinkedWorking

LinkedWorking is a great rubber meets the road to networking on LinkedIn. Lewis and Frank have taken a straight-to-the-point approach to online networking and how it will expand your horizons professionally and personally. I highly recommend you read and act on the advice in this book

Gary Unger, Author
"How To Be A Creative Genius (in five minutes or less)"

We are living in some pretty extraordinary times in that the internet, the social media revolution and advances in networking communications have drastically and permanently changed human evolution into a HUMAN REVOLUTION and LinkedIn is certainly one of the contributing factors to this phenomenon. And while we have yet to understand the long-lasting effects this will have on humanity, this book continues such a necessary discussion.

Adam J. Kovitz, CEO & Founder of The National Networker

In this day and age, one can never be 'too connected' - and LinkedIn has been a tremendous tool for me in building new friendships & business relationships.

This book, with its marvelous collection of LinkedIn success stories, will serve as inspiration to others out there, who have yet to experience this for themselves.

Stan Relihan, President & CEO of Expert Executive Search

True networkers recognize their own. Frank is in an elite class who continues to give and give. Those who are fortunate enough to make his acquaintance, even if just through the stories he tells in this book, will instantly realize what a gift he is to us all.

Terry Bean, Founder of Motor City Connect

LINKEDWORKING™

Generating Success on the
World's Largest Professional Networking Website

PRESS

418 Press
A Division of Four Eighteen Enterprises, LLC
Post Office Box 30724,
Columbus, Ohio 43230

Ordering Information:

To order additional copies, contact your local bookstore. For
quantity discounts contact 418 Press at the address listed
above.

418 Press Logo Design: Jessica Moreland (Columbus, Ohio)
Book Cover: New City Graphics (Columbus, Ohio)
Editing and Interior Design: Paul Holland (Cleveland, Ohio)
Proofreading: Jennifer Eller (Rockford, Illinois)

To

Frances Jackson and Diana Howes

... Our mothers.

Need we say any more?

FIRST NEW ALLIANCE DICTIONARY

link[1] (liŋk) *n.* **1.** any of a series of rings or loops making up a chain. **2.** a) a section of some thing resembling a chain [a link of sausage] b) a point or stage in a series of circumstances [a weak *link* in the evidence] **3.** *same as* CUFF LINK **4.** anything serving to connect

link·age (lin'kij) *n.* **1.** a linking or being liked **2.** a series or system of links; esp., a series of connecting rods for transmitting power or motion **3.** *Biol.* The tendency of some genes to remain together and act as a unit (**linkage group**) in inheritance, generally in the same chromosome, without segregation throughout maturation

link·boy (-boi') *n.* a boy or man formerly hired to carry a link, or torch, to light one's way at night: also *link'man* (-m_n), pl. - **men** (-m_ən)

link·ed·work·ing (link'wur'kin) *vi.* the process of conducting professional networking on *LinkedIn*, the world's largest professional networking website *-n.* the title of the highly useful book written by Frank Agin and Lewis Howes that shows readers how to generate opportunities, contacts and success using LinkedIn.

link·up (liŋk'up') *n.* a joining together of two objects, factions, interests, etc.

link·work (liŋk'wurk') *n.* **1.** anything made in links, as a chain **2.** a gear system operating by links

FOREWORD

Work isn't "going to change." It has changed. Did you?

If you're in the camp that thinks LinkedIn is the online representation of your resume, Frank and Lewis are here to set you straight. Your goal, over the next several pages, is to read voraciously, shake your head in astonishment, and make a big fat action list of what you have to do the moment you finish reading this book.

It's that important.

The information in this book is a mix of case studies, stories, and how-to, all wrapped in the strategy points you'll need to understand where it all comes from. It's all laid out on a platter for you. At this point, you need only read along, feel sheepish, and change how you're approaching your business.

Employers, you need to enable and empower this. No more hoarding. Your employees are far more powerful when they become LinkedWorkers. You know that HR and career paths have been shaky for the last several years. In this economy, who's putting money into the future growth of employees? Don't delude yourself. Let your employees power up using this book as a starting point.

FOREWARD (cont)

I'm not a futurist. I'm someone who reads the trends and applies them to today's business challenges. This, my friends, is a central business challenge of today. If you're not valuing small, powerful networks, you're already dead and you don't know it.

Here's a chance at rebirth. Take it. Please?

Chris Brogan
January 23, 2009

Chris Brogan is the co-author of *Trust Agents* (with Julien Smith) and is President of New Marketing Labs, a new media marketing agency, as well as the home of the New Marketing Summit conferences and New Marketing Bootcamp educational events. He helps large and mid-sized businesses understand how to use social media tools like blogging, social networks, community platforms, and more to build business value for marketers, sales organizations, and internal collaboration in general. For more information on this, please contact him directly at chris@chrisbrogan.com or read his blog at [chrisbrogan.com].

TABLE OF CONTENTS

An Introduction To LinkedWorking

"LinkedIn doesn't work!" This is what I (far too often) hear when I talk to people about the world's largest online professional networking site. As of February 2009, LinkedIn has over 30 millions users and it adds tens of thousand every day. Yet, I get the sense that the vast majority are perplexed as to how they can use it to create opportunities for themselves. As a result, they lash out in complete exasperation whenever someone mentions this website, "LinkedIn doesn't work" or other similar phrases.

LinkedIn does work, however. I know that it does. How I know this is that in a relatively short period, and without a tremendous investment of time, I created many wonderful professional opportunities for myself using LinkedIn.

While I did not get on to LinkedIn until late in 2007, it is important to give you a complete picture so you can see just much LinkedIn has done for me.

In the spring of 2007, I had an opportunity to fulfill a childhood dream. After a highly successful career in high school and college football, I earned a spot on an arena football team. This is simply football played indoors during the spring and summer months and serves as a training or proving ground for those vying to play in the National Football League.

During the second game of the season, I dove to catch the football. Unfortunately, however, I slammed into the walls that surround the playing surface in arena football and severely broke my wrist.

While I finished out the season with my hand taped, at the end of the season I took the team doctor's advice and had surgery. The surgery turned out to be more complicated than anyone imagined. They literally had to take a piece of bone from my hip and fuse it to my wrist bone.

What was only supposed to be a few weeks in a cast turned into over six months in a cast, and then another six months of rehabilitation.

At first the situation caused me to be without focus, depressed and unmotivated. Eventually however, I realized that I needed to make something of myself. While my dream of playing professional football may have been temporarily, and possibly permanently, sidetracked, I resolved that I would pursue other things.

As the full cast I was in prevented me from working, I decided to complete my undergraduate degree at Capital University in Columbus, Ohio. In addition, I resolved to work on various aspects of personal development. This included developing my leadership skills, becoming a capable professional speaker and being more proficient with the Internet.

In the late fall of 2007, while surfing the Internet and playing with e-mail, Stuart Jenkins sent me a request to join him on LinkedIn. At the time, I knew nothing of LinkedIn. I might have deleted Stuart's request, but for two things. First, Stuart was not just anyone, he was a former lead figure at Principia College in Elsah, Illinois, a successful inventor and entrepreneur, a motivational speaker and someone who had great friendships with just about every major player in the sports industry.

Second, I had vowed to immerse myself in learning how to make more of the Internet. Here was something I knew nothing about, but if LinkedIn was something with which Stuart was involved, then I knew it was something I needed to explore.

I accepted Stuart's invitation and began playing with LinkedIn. Every day, I learned a little more about this website. I tinkered with the various features on LinkedIn and just as Stuart had invited me join him, I started inviting others that I knew to become part of my network on LinkedIn.

Then, in February of 2008, while exploring one of the features on LinkedIn, I decided to create a group. Playing off my childhood dream, I created the Professional Athlete Network. Once LinkedIn officially sanctioned the group, I began inviting people that I knew who were associated with professional athletics (such as Stuart Jenkins, teammates from arena football and others I had met in my travels) and I encouraged them to invite others that they knew.

While it started slowly, within a couple months this group had a membership of several hundred people and it was growing by the dozens every day. These members were not just football players. They were from every imaginable sport and not just from the United States, they were from all over the world.

As the central figure in a very large and rapidly growing network of professional athletes and related industries, opportunities seemed to find me. In April 2008, after conversations with several professional athletes, and helping them connect with others, a promoter sent me an invitation for an all-expense paid trip to play in a charity soccer game in the New York Giants stadium involving celebrities and professional athletes.

I gladly accepted and had the opportunity to play soccer with and against the likes of all-pro NFL football players and Hollywood A-list figures.

Then in May, another connection invited me to meet him in southern California. He was a former National Football League player working to place football players in commercials and movies. He then introduced me to his agent, who connected me with the director of a reality television program, as well as a writer for Universal Studios. These people offered me help in finding work in commercials and movies.

As part of that trip, I met with Stuart Jenkins (my original LinkedIn contact) who then offered me a job opportunity working for a new branch of a major shoe company he operated.

In addition, I met with another person I met via LinkedIn who was casting for a reality show for aspiring professional football players. While no one has picked up the show yet, the basis of the reality program is that the winner of the show would receive a guaranteed arena football contract, and possibly a contract with a team in the National Football League. Based on what he knew of me from LinkedIn, he felt I would be a perfect candidate for the show and that it would be great exposure for me.

On this same trip, I flew back through New York City to attend an event to which another LinkedIn contact invited me. Called the "The Ultimate Athlete Challenge," *Men's Fitness Magazine* hosted this event. At the event, I met and spoke with the editor in chief of the magazine. In addition, someone from *Men's Fitness* interviewed me for a new show called "How to Become an Ultimate Athlete."

While in New York City this second time, I met with another LinkedIn connection who asked me to help him create an All-Star Arena Football game in Europe, that would pit a European team against one from the United States.

Beyond sports, television and related events, during the downtime from my surgery and the resulting rehabilitation, I designed a couple of products that I planned to develop and market. Through LinkedIn, I met a product designer who expressed an interested in working with me on these projects.

From here the list of opportunities from LinkedIn continues to cascade towards me. I have received numerous free trips around the country and I was retained to assist with a sports industry magazine. I have been presented with countless sponsorship and product licensing opportunities with commissions worth tens of thousands of dollars and was given free ad space and booths for various prominent trade shows around the country.   These things inspired me to launch my own blog and online newsletter, *The Sports Networker.*

All these opportunities are ones that I have created while being on LinkedIn. This begs the questions ... Why did LinkedIn work for me when so many others struggle to find success on LinkedIn? To be honest, before I embarked on writing this book, my answer would have been, "I don't know." Seriously, I found many opportunities through LinkedIn, but I did not know how or why.

Frankly, that bothered me. While I enjoyed success, I knew it would not last. Thus, I needed to create more opportunities (after all, one All-Star Arena Football game would not make an entire career). Yet, I was uncertain as to whether or not I could duplicate my success on LinkedIn.

Then one day, while perplexed by this dilemma, I had lunch with Frank Agin. Frank is someone I met in October of 2007 through our mutual involvement in Toastmasters, and he is the founder and president of AmSpirit Business Connections, a national organization that empowers entrepreneurs, sales representatives and professionals to become more successful through networking and developing stronger business relationships.

While growing AmSpirit Business Connections, Frank has established himself as an authority on professional networking and business relationship development. He has written dozens of articles on professional networking.

Frank also wrote the book *Foundational Networking: Building Know, Like and Trust To Create A Lifetime of Extraordinary Success.*

At lunch, I asked Frank his opinion as to why I achieved so much success creating opportunities through LinkedIn (while others seemingly struggle to even just build contacts). He pulled out a pad and paper. Together we then detailed my various activities and efforts on LinkedIn.

Frank asked several questions and took many notes. When he was done, he put down his pen and began to give me insights into my success, on which I will allow him to elaborate in his own words ...

There is no question that Lewis has generated great success on LinkedIn. In fact, many of you would deem it enviable success. The main reason Lewis created opportunities on LinkedIn, and will continue to do so, is that he uses it to network and not as a substitute for networking.

Here is the problem. Every time there is some new technological feature, many people think that they can use it to circumvent the networking process.

In short, they conclude that the technology will make networking obsolete. For example: With the advent of the telephone (whether mobile telephones or landlines), far too many business people believed they could achieve quick results via telemarketing or simply "working the phone." Even before "Do Not Call" list legislation stymied these business types, the telephone did nothing to displace good old fashioned networking.

Along came cheap and easy e-mail, and many of the same people turned to mass e-mailing programs of one sort or another to level the playing field against traditional networking. Even before SPAM filters, it did not work.

Now there is LinkedIn and people have come to it by the millions thinking - and in many cases hoping - that it is a quick fix or shortcut to their networking deficiencies or aversions. As good as LinkedIn is, it will not triumph over networking.

Networking is as human a trait as there is. Every human networks - no matter the region, culture or religion. It is what we do. Humans have been networking since the beginning of our time on this planet.

Early humans found that their chances of survival increased if they worked together. However, they were only willing to work with one another if they knew one another, liked one another and trusted one another. These elements only manifested themselves when there was a genuine relationship. Thus, only those early humans who were adept at creating relationships ultimately survived.

Know, like and trust were (and still are) the elements of successful interaction. They have been part of the human species for literally hundreds of thousands of years. A mere hundred years of telecommunications does not negate the human need for relationships and the "know, like and trust" behind them (neither will a couple decades of e-mails or a few years of LinkedIn).

So how Lewis created opportunities on LinkedIn was a matter of him creating an environment of "know, like and trust" on LinkedIn. In simple terms, his actions and activities on LinkedIn were consistent with what most of us practice, or should be practicing, when we network in the real world.

LinkedIn is a powerful networking tool (as is the telephone and e-mail). It is not, however, a replacement for networking. So, this book is not about how to use LinkedIn - there are already plenty of books that will give you a nuts-n-bolts primer on LinkedIn as well as the FAQ section on the website itself.

This book is about LinkedWorking, as we term it - networking on LinkedIn. It is for those who have a general understanding of the workings of LinkedIn, and want to be more successful working LinkedIn to create opportunities.

Each chapter of this book will do three things. First, Frank Agin will share a real world networking practice that has proven itself to be effective in creating traditional networking opportunities and success. His knowledge of, and experience related to networking in the "real world" will create a frame of reference from which you can change your LinkedIn experience.

Then Lewis Howes will explain how he used the features of LinkedIn (even though he may not have known it at the time) to mimic the real world networking practice to create opportunities through his LinkedIn contacts.

Whether you seek to become a globally recognized leader or just a regional subject matter thought leader, Lewis' experiences will help create a LinkedIn game plan for you to create exciting opportunities, expand your business and ultimately make money. In addition, he will share a number of tricks and tips that he picked up and developed using LinkedIn.

Finally, we will share with you other success stories of people who have also used the features of LinkedIn to create opportunities for themselves. Lewis has had great success on LinkedIn. He, however, is not alone. Among the millions and millions of people on LinkedIn, there are dozens and dozens who have achieved great success finding opportunities, making contacts and building businesses.

Remember LinkedIn is a great tool for networking, but it is not a replacement for networking itself. That is important to bear in mind as you read on.

SEE OPPORTUNITIES IN EVERYONE

*"Let your hook always be cast; in the pool
where you least expect it, there will be a fish."*

Ovid

REAL WORLD NETWORKING LESSON

You have been guilty of this at one time or another -
disregarded someone as having little or no influence on your
life. If you are honest with yourself, you will admit this. You
do not need to admit it to anyone but yourself. While it is not
laudable behavior, at some point everyone has been guilty of
this. So go ahead and admit it.

It may have been an administrative staff person at work
or at a client's office. It may have been the attendant at the
dry cleaner or gas station. It may even have been the person
delivering the newspaper or a college student working to be
able to return to school. Whomever the person and whatever
the situation, the level of attention and respect you afforded
this person does not compare to that which you gave to say,
your boss, a key client or a close friend.

Why would it? They hold no sway in your life. They will
not get you that next job, promotion or pay raise. They will
not be responsible for contributing revenue to your bottom
line or adding clients to your portfolio. They will not provide
you with continued acceptance in, or admittance to, any sort
of social circles.

As you felt that nothing would come from it, you did not
feel as if you needed to invest a commensurate amount of
attention and respect in them. So, perhaps you snubbed them
by failing to say hello, please or thank you. Or perhaps you
ignored them altogether, completely failing to make eye contact.

Whatever the case, when you disregard someone, you lose. No matter the motivation, by avoiding a relationship you squander networking potential.

While it is true that not everyone has the potential to be your new employer, next great client or star employee, it is also true that everyone knows someone that could. For that reason, every contact has opportunity.

You do not know from where your next great job or client will come. You do not know from where your next great contact will come. You do not know who will provide you the information that will give you the edge over the competition. So what do you do? **Simple. You treat everyone the same.**

In my book *Foundational Networking*, I shared a story about my consistent friendly interaction with Twyla, the attendant where I parked my car. From this, Twyla referred me to an opportunity to be an extra in the movie *The Shawshank Redemption*. I could not have ever known that this would be the result of a daily hello and cordial chitchat as I handed over the keys to my car each morning.

You need to make it a habit to have eye contact with, smile at and say hello to everyone you encounter. From this, if a conversation ensues, then embrace it. Take a moment to invest some time in that person.

Listen to what they have to say. This will provide clues as to how you can help them. More importantly, this will give you insights in to how they might be able to help you.

Have compassion for their situation. No one is where he or she wants to be. Everyone wants more out of life. Maybe there is something simple you can do to get them there, even if it is only feeling important because you spent a moment with them.

If they boast of an achievement or personal triumph, be excited for them. Even if it seems to be trivial relative to your stature in life, realize that this person has worked hard to accomplish what they have. Make them feel good about it.

Assume the attitude that you are not above interacting with any one. This is not to suggest that you need to invite the paperboy to your holiday party or have the gas station attendant over for the big game. It does suggest, however, that you need to treat everyone with the same attention and respect as you would a new employer, great client or star employee - because somehow or another everyone is connected to one of those people.

APPLYING THE LESSON TO LINKEDIN

Have you received one of those generic invitations to connect on LinkedIn? You know, the one that looks like:

If you have not, you will soon. If you are like me, it will become one of your biggest cyber pet peeves.

I understand it if someone is new to the system and has not yet discovered LinkedIn etiquette. However, it is annoying to receive these impersonal invitations to connect from complete strangers.

Luckily, you have a decision to make. You have two primary choices: You can choose not to accept by ignoring the message or by clicking on the "Archive" button. Or you can click on the "I Don't Know This Person" button.

Fortunately, if you receive a generic invitation in your inbox, you have a real opportunity. It is to simply ask them how they came across your profile and why exactly they wanted to connect. If they do not send you a response then you may want to consider not connecting. Most likely they will reply with an answer, giving you a chance to create mutually beneficial opportunities.

I would say that close to 75 percent of the invitations I receive are generic with no personal touch. Does it annoy me? Yes. Nevertheless, I usually send a brief note thanking them for the connection, asking how they came across my profile and if there is anything I can do to help. This leaves it up to them to respond and with any reasonable response, I will accept their invitation.

When you send an invitation you should always try to make it personal, or at least add some value to the message. Here is a great example of a brief, yet personal, message I received that I was completely comfortable accepting:

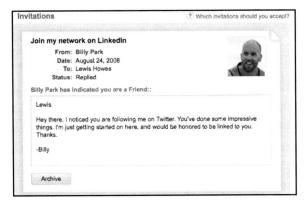

A personal touch like the example above always increases your chances of being accepted. You will not always receive these personal invitations, but it will be in your best interest to see the opportunities in everyone.

For example, let me share with you my encounter with Anne Marie Principe. When Anne Marie tried to join one of my exclusive groups, The Professional Athlete Network, she also sent me a generic invitation to join her personal network. I sent her an e-mail stating that she would not be able to join because I did not see that she was a professional athlete, nor had worked for professional athletes. Her title simply read "Executive Director, The Books for Kids Foundation". I thought she just worked for a book foundation.

What I did not know was that she was an event planner for a number of large charity events that many high profile professional athletes attend. After she sent me a thoughtful e-mail back explaining all of this, I gladly accepted her in the group.

After trading a few e-mails worth of introductions and small talk I learned that one of her objectives was finding celebrities and professional athletes to attend events in hopes of drawing in more attendees, sponsors and donations. Her main purpose for joining the Professional Athlete Network on LinkedIn was to connect with other professional athletes through the group and have them come to an upcoming event.

With this knowledge, I was able to introduce her to several athletes who ended up attending. In addition, I connected her to several sports philanthropy individuals to help with finding sponsors for the event.

Anne Marie was so appreciative of the introductions that she invited me to come attend the event. She was even able to get a sponsor to pay for my trip. Attending this event opened many doors for me and served to further connect me with other professional athletes, celebrities, sportscasters, and former sports icons.

You never know how these connections will come in handy in the future. This is why it is important to never pass judgment while on LinkedIn. Yes, the logic is obvious to reach out to some "Power Users" and "Mega Networkers" but it is also important to connect with certain individuals who send generic invitations and have incomplete profiles, because you never know what they have to offer.

SUCCESS STORY

Stan Relihan, President and CEO, Expert Executive Search

Podcast: http://connections.thepodcastnetwork.co
LinkedIn: www.LinkedIn.com/in/stanrelihan
Web site: www.expertsearch.com.au

Stan Relihan is a headhunter and recruiter based in Sydney, Australia, with more than 10 years of success in assisting start-ups, blue chip multi-nationals and leading regional players in satisfying their human capital requirements.

With a background in advertising and media, he was involved in the genesis of the Internet and broadband access in Australia and maintains a strong interest and involvement in the world of digital media and technology.

Now, as Asia Pacific's most-connected LinkedIn user (and in the Top 50 worldwide), Stan is also the host of The Connections Show, one of the world's most popular business podcasts - and is an acknowledged expert in Web 2.0 and social networking.

HIS STORY ... HIS WORDS

I first joined LinkedIn in April 2005, mostly out of solidarity with the person that had invited me - and then promptly forgot about it. A year later though, a friend of mine, who'd been reading Malcolm Gladwell's book *The Tipping Point*, was so inspired by the book that he sent me his personal copy for me to read.

I'm a recruiter. In the over 10 years I'd been in the business, I have never filled a full-time position through advertising. Rather, I'd always relied on the process of networking, research and detective work to find my candidates.

I'd always prided myself on my network and my abilities as a networker - but reading *The Tipping Point* was an eye-opening experience for me.

It showed me that for all my skills, I was only scratching the surface of potential opportunities that were available through more widespread interactions with other people - both physical and virtual.

This catalyzed me to start actively building my LinkedIn network - mainly through a process of inviting people in my Outlook address book, as well as looking for people on LinkedIn that were open to receiving invitations from strangers - Open Networkers, as many described themselves.

Before long, I found myself (rather surprisingly), to be Australia's 'Most-connected LinkedIn User,' with around 5,000 first-degree connections. As a result, in April 2007 I was interviewed on Cameron Reilly's *G'Day World* show on The Podcast Network, on the subject of 'Using LinkedIn as a Business Tool.' During the interview, Cameron (who was a real LinkedIn skeptic), issued me a challenge: Use my LinkedIn Network to find the most impressive celebrity guest I could find to appear on his show. This was a real test of the quality and depth of the LinkedIn network, as well as the willingness of the LinkedIn community to help with introductions.

I'm pleased to report that as a result none other than Vint Cerf, (co-inventor of the Internet and Chief Internet Evangelist at Google) appeared as a guest about six weeks later.

As funny as this may sound, in relative terms, this was still the beginning for me. I started routinely reaching out to whomever and accepting invitations from whomever asked. I was never prejudiced towards anyone who invited me to connect or anyone I encountered.

As a result of this approach and through all these connections, I now have my own weekly podcast show on business networking and Web 2.0, called Connections (http://connections.thepodcastnetwork.com), which attracts over 15,000 downloads per month.

In addition to the many new friends and business relationships I've developed (both with the guests that appear on the show as well as listeners that have written to me), as a result of this exposure, I now receive between 50 and 100 invitations to connect with people on LinkedIn each day ... seven days a week ... 365 days a year.

This approach to connecting on LinkedIn has catapulted me onto the list of 'Top 50' LinkedIn Power Users (http://www.toplinked.com/top50.html), with well over 25,000 direct connections - which, needless to say, is very useful for me in my capacity as a recruiter.

Considering that I'm located in a remote corner of the globe in Sydney, Australia and just a few years ago had only 175 connections, this is a profound testimony to the power of LinkedIn, networking in general and building a personal brand in the online world.

SUMMARY

No matter who you encounter and no matter where you encounter them, there is an opportunity. It might not be direct. It might not be immediate. It might not be obvious. Nevertheless, there is an opportunity.

IDENTIFY CAPSTONES AND WEAK TIES

"The life I touch for good or ill will touch another life, and that in turn another, until who knows where the trembling stops or in what far place my touch will be felt."

Frederick Buechner

REAL WORLD NETWORKING LESSON

Everyone is a networking opportunity for you (and you are an opportunity for everyone). This is a powerful networking concept. As powerful as it is, however, there are limitations to it. The primary limitation is that you have no control over where this networking strategy leads. That is, you can never tell when you will come across a networking opportunity and when you do, you have little control as to what might be.

You eliminate much of this limitation when you take it upon yourself to reconnect with people. This is also a powerful networking concept as they presumably already know, like and trust you. The issue you need to address with this, however, is figuring out where to start. If you are like most, there are dozens, if not hundreds, of people with whom you can reconnect - individuals from school, career and community activities, just to list a few.

If you are interested in taking an active approach to networking and making the best use of your time networking, you should identify those people in your network who are *Capstones* and *Weak Ties*.

Capstones

In the 1960's, social psychologist, Stanley Milgram, conducted a series of studies generally referred to as the "small world" problem. In one such study, he sent to 160 randomly selected individuals in Omaha, Nebraska, a packet with the name and address of a stockbroker who lived and worked near Boston.

Milgram instructed each individual to send the packet to the individual listed. If, however, they did not know the individual, they were to write their name on the roster in the packet and then mail the packet to a friend or acquaintance who they thought would get it to the stockbroker (or at least closer). This was to continue until the packet actually reached the Boston stockbroker.

Eventually, all the packets arrived to the stockbroker. Some packets made the journey in as little as two steps and others in as many as 10. On average, however, the packets reached the broker in about six steps. This led to the initial theorization that everyone is linked to everyone else in just six steps (thus Milgram coined the phrase "six degrees of separation").

In reviewing the results, Milgram noticed that many of the chain packets followed the same asymmetrical pattern. In all, over half of the packets that got to the stockbroker were delivered by three people. Hence, Milgram revised his "six degrees of separation" theory to state that while you may not be personally six degrees away from the rest of the world, you likely know someone who is. Hence you are linked to the rest of the world through these power connectors.

Applying this to the real world, if you are interested in maximizing your networking efforts, you are well advised to devote time and attention to these power connectors in your network. This begs the question ... Who are they?

While much science went into these theories, there is a relatively practical way to identify your power connectors. Write down the names of 40 people you know. These should be friends, acquaintances and colleagues, but not blood relatives. Then for each of these people, determine who introduced you to that person ... and who introduced you to that person ... and who introduced you to that person.

As you do this for your 40 friends, acquaintances and colleagues, a pattern will begin to emerge. In fact, if you graphically map out your network, this exercise will reveal that what you term as your social circles is really just a pyramid. That is, a large percentage of your contacts originated from a relatively few number of individuals. Those individuals at the tops of these pyramids, which is known as the capstone, are your power connectors.

If you are looking to make the most of your networking efforts, focus your time and energy on any or all of your Capstones. Take them to lunch, breakfast, coffee - or other social activity. These individuals have been instrumental in building your network to this point. It is likely they will do more of the same in the future. Invest in them.

Weak Ties

While Capstones are a great networking resource, there is also power in relationships that are not close at all.

In his 1974 book, *Getting A Job*, sociologist Mark Granovetter indicated that through his research he found that 56 percent of people found jobs through personal contacts. This is not surprising, as most jobs are never even officially posted.

The surprise in his research, however, was that the personal contacts used to obtain these jobs were generally not from family or close friends. Rather the most effective contacts were those Granovetter referred to as "weak ties." According to Granovetter, of the individuals who reported that they found a job through personal contacts, 55.6 percent said that they saw their contact only occasionally and 27.8 percent indicated they saw their contact only rarely.

Therefore, when it comes to finding out about new jobs - or, for that matter, most anything related to networking - your weak ties tend to be more important than strong ones. This is so because your close ties tend to occupy the same world as you do. Your family, friends and co-workers often know many of the same people you do.

On the other hand, mere acquaintances are much more likely to know something that you do not. Thus, some of the most important people in your life are those who are not close to you. In fact, to a degree the more people you know who are not close to you the stronger your position becomes.

Thus, a great means of fortifying your network is to make a point of occasionally associating with people you know, but not that well. Certainly, having lunch with the person in the next office or cubicle is comfortable and it can be fun. However, it does little to build your network.

If you want to build your network, have lunch with that person with whom you are only somewhat acquainted - the person who occupies the office or cubicle down the hall or in the building three blocks away. While this effort may take you somewhat out of your comfort zone, from a networking perspective it will prove more productive.

APPLYING THE LESSON TO LINKEDIN

Certainly, I benefit from every connection. As I began to really look at where many of my opportunities came from, it was hard to deny that there are patterns similar to what Frank discusses.

Amongst my close connections, there are those capstones that seem to come through (directly and indirectly) time after time, and have a consistent ongoing impact on my LinkedIn network. Outside of my capstones, I also seem to generate a fair amount of information, ideas and introductions from those I have known, but not so well as to call them a close connection.

Certainly, the concept of capstones and weak ties is also powerful on LinkedIn. As such, there are five ways to create value for and to generate benefit from your capstones:

Capstones

1. **Stay Connected:** Be sure to write an e-mail, make a comment, send a text or call at least once every two weeks to remain fresh in their minds and continue to build the know, like and trust.

2. **Introduce:** Make quality introductions to individuals who they will benefit from the most. Go out of your way to recommend that they get in touch with another person you are connected with, and they will soon realize you are someone worth helping more often.

3. **Stop The SPAM:** Do not forward "spammy like" introductions to capstones or you risk losing the trust of your capstones. Rather send an e-mail in reply to the alluded spammer stating that you would rather not forward it along due to the time constraints of your capstone, (but offer to them help with something else instead).

4. **Link Love:** Add a link to them on your "status update", or pose a question that promotes their website. As free promotion is anyone's friend, this will move you up on their "connections" radar.

5. **Make It Personal:** There is nothing more powerful then sending a meaningful note that expresses your appreciation for all someone has done. If you do not already have your capstone's personal mailing address, then ask for it and send a card or gift in the mail. Make it personal and you will be happy with the results.

Likewise, there are five ways to create value for and to generate benefit from your weak ties:

Weak Ties

1. **Stay Connected:** Endeavour to stay connected with the weak ties with e-mails or newsletters. You never know if they have a consulting gig, or job offering that is perfect for you.

2. **Reply to E-mail:** No matter how many e-mails you receive each day, you can still reply to your weak ties with brief responses. If you are strapped for time then keep it to one sentence, or write to tell them you will respond later.

3. **Spread Connections:** Not all connections send introductions that are "spammy." Some of them are trying to gain quality relationships or they have a great offer to benefit one of your connections. Learn to recognize the fake from the fabulous, and forward along the introductions that are mutually beneficial.

4. **Be Altruistic:** Go through your network and pick out two or three connections that you may not know that well, but would like to know better. Pick out an article online pertaining to their business and send them a link along with a friendly note. This will show them that you take the time to think about them and are open to building a stronger connection.

5. **Follow Through:** If you offer to do something, it is a big mistake to not follow through. If you say you will make an introduction, or provide useful help then be sure to do exactly as you say.

SUCCESS STORY

Terry Bean, Founder, Motor City Connect and Networked Inc.
Website: www.networkedinc.com
LinkedIn: www.LinkedIn.com/in/terrybean

Terry's passion is helping others succeed. As a consummate networker, he makes sure he understands not only the needs of his associates, but how to bring together the required resources to satisfy those needs.

Terry is the driving force behind Networked Inc., a company that he co-founded to bring buyers and sellers of products and services together efficiently. His firm has provided training on the concepts and benefits of networking to numerous sales teams and professionals.

Terry holds a B.S. in Psychology and a M.A. in Business Communications from Eastern Michigan University. He enjoys playing softball, weight training, watching The Simpsons and playing with his daughter, Drea.

HIS STORY ... HIS WORDS

I have been an active networker since 1995, when I first met Frank Agin in what is now AmSpirit Business Connections. The idea of helping others and having them help me instantly made sense to me. I now run the fastest growing networking group in Detroit, write for a national publication and am a sought after speaker on topics related to building better business relationships and managing social capital.

LinkedIn has played a tremendous part in this. Moreover, my success from LinkedIn is attributed to how well I use it as a tool, and that can all be linked to one person.

I joined LinkedIn back in November 2004, after I had received my third invite in a two-week span. Interestingly, it was an invitation from Gina Winterstein, one of my capstones in Columbus, Ohio, that finally motivated me to take action. You see, the first two people who had invited me were friends, and not necessarily folks who I considered networking experts.

I am sure that my first four months on LinkedIn were like those of most. I set-up a bleak profile and sent an invite to join to a handful of friends. Then I basically waited for LinkedIn to deliver. Guess what? It didn't. Not surprisingly, at that point I wasn't sure about the value of LinkedIn.

I remember having a conversation with a capstone of mine in Detroit, Dave Biskner, about his experience with LinkedIn. Dave is a truth-seeker, so I knew he would dive in deeper than I had. His response confirmed what I had believed: LinkedIn was of limited usefulness (although, at this time LinkedIn didn't quite have two million members).

Then a very interesting thing happened in March 2005 (at least, at the time it was interesting as I didn't yet have the benefit of hindsight on my side). Dave sent me a link to the profile of Vincent Wright from Connecticut. I remember reading Vincent's profile and thinking, "WOW, this guy is a lot like me".

I immediately sent Vincent a request to converse and he quickly responded. While Vincent acknowledged our similarities, he did something so much more than that. He asked how he could help me. I was used to that in the face-to-face world of networking, but that was the first time I had experienced it online. That was inspiring. He then introduced me to a forum he created called "my LinkedIn power forum" (MLPF), which is now known as "my virtual power forum" (www.myvirtualpowerforum.com).

He created MLPF to help his friends and associates make better use of LinkedIn ... and make better use of it I did. Through MLPF I met great people all over the world, many with more than 15 years of networking experience. Who knew that people were doing this online back in the early 1990's? Through reading the posts and connecting with these interesting folks, I not only learned about LinkedIn, I was growing my network.

A few months later I found a group called LIONs (which in an acronym for LinkedIn Open Networkers ... although I often joke that it should stand for: Lazy In Our Networking). Their premise is simple, if you want to grow your network fast and were open to doing it with people you don't know, LIONs was the place to be. These are the folks who have thousands of connections on LinkedIn. While this isn't a group you can go to and ask for a lot of personal introductions to their network, it is one where you can find a lot of people through their network. These folks are generally willing to help you connect with anyone, even though they aren't in a position of influence with them. These folks are and have weak ties, but lots of them.

The ability to see and be seen through the LinkedIn network is directly proportional to the number of connections one has. The more connections, the more likely you are to find what you seek when searching (as well as be found when others are searching). As an open networker, I firmly believe that connections lead to opportunities and opportunities lead to the need for more connections.

As such, I quickly learned how to connect with the top connectors on LinkedIn. To do this, there's a great little technique I teach people when I train them on how to use LinkedIn. Most of them are happy to learn this. For you, I suggest that you invite Ron Bates (San Francisco, California) to join your network. If LinkedIn had an official capstone, he would likely be in the running.

I remember hitting 100 connections in LinkedIn back in September 2005. It was a big day for me. At that point, I still had a lot more outstanding invitations than accepted. Fast forward to present and it's a very different story. While I don't send a lot of invites, the ones I do send are going to people who have a 95% chance of having heard of LinkedIn (unlike back in 2005 when very few people had heard of it). They accept them readily and are pleased that we have joined networks.

Through my capstones and weak ties on LinkedIn I have had many opportunities and experiences, a few of which include:

- Launch www.motorcityconnect.com and make it the premiere networking group in Detroit, Michigan.
- Be Appointed the Social Networking Editor for www.thenationalnetworker.com.
- Identify talent for 32 markets around the United States when I was the corporate recruiter for what is now Cavalier Telephone.
- Became part of the Relationship Networking Industry Association and help it define itself and the metrics it needed to classify networking as an industry.
- Became a sought after speaker and trainer, being engaged to do both numerous times each month on the topics related to networking and LinkedIn.
- Land new clients like www.curvedetroit.com, www.urefer.com, and www.facilitymatrix.com.
- Became a better facilitator of conversation due to the numerous groups I have moderated.
- Became the "go to" guy for people in my network when they are seeking any type of resource or simply need to know more about LinkedIn.

I am a networker who is very interested in helping others. If I were to honestly look at my over several-thousand person LinkedIn network, I could not tell you a story about more than a third of them. Why? The reason is that for some I am a capstone, but for the vast majority of others I am just a weak tie.

The important point is that when you know who each is in your network, you get to do what I define in networking as: "Leverage the relationships you have to create the relationships you need."

SUMMARY

It is important to build the foundation of networking - know, like and trust - with your capstones and weak ties. Whether in the real world or on LinkedIn, each has the ability to create your next big opportunity and in all likelihood, will.

LinkedWorking

LEAD A LIFE OF ALTRUISM

"The wise man does not lay up his own treasures. The more he gives to others, the more he has for his own."
Lao Tzu

REAL WORLD NETWORKING LESSON

Networking is nothing more than two or more people cooperating to benefit one another through the exchange of opportunities, information, support, energy and additional contacts. If you are looking to improve the flow of these benefits, I advise you to first focus your efforts on providing these benefits to individuals in your network.

Yes, this is somewhat counterintuitive. You network to get, but to prime the pump of this getting, you have to give first. This is the Golden Rule of Networking: Give first ... get second.

Donna Fisher, in her book *People Power,* refers to this as the "Boomerang Effect." According to Fisher, taking the initiative to give, participate and offer support to your network is similar to throwing a boomerang. Eventually what you inject into your network - opportunities, information, support, energy and additional contacts - comes back to you.

Why does the "boomerang effect" work? Remember the last time someone did you a favor? Perhaps they gave a lead on a new employee or produced unique information related to your industry. Whatever the favor, you certainly said, "thank you" and maybe even sent a gift basket.

Despite these gestures of gratitude, you probably still felt an underlying sense of obligation. This is because most people have a difficult time receiving and not giving back. It is this aspect of human nature that serves to provide the drive that returns the "boomerang" to the giver.

It is important to note that you can never predict when these boomerangs or acts of altruism will come back to you. Sometimes it occurs immediately. Sometimes you wait days; other times weeks, and still other times you can wait years. Because you cannot predict their return, however, you should not expect it. We just need to trust that what you give out will come back.

Consider the case of Mexico as documented by Robert Cialdini, Ph.D. in his book *Instant Influence.* In 1990, after Mexico City suffered a disastrous earthquake, the government of Mexico received a $5,000 contribution from Ethiopia.

This was puzzling to Cialdini. After all, at this same time, Ethiopia was in the midst of a terrible famine. On a daily basis its people were literally dying by the hundreds. Why would Ethiopia not keep the $5,000 for use with its own people?

When asked this very question, the Ethiopian Relief Agency simply responded, "In 1935, when Italy invaded, Mexico helped us." In this case, Mexico could not have predicted when it would need a return of support. Therefore, it would have been senseless to expect it. Ethiopia's return of support over 50 years later simply serves as confirmation that if we give and trust in the Golden Rule of Networking, opportunities, information, support, energy and additional contacts will come back to us from our network.

Given that giving without expectation to your networking is a surefire formula for reaping benefits from those around you, you need to surrender to this notion and find every opportunity you can to give to others.

The starting point or foundation for this mindset is being thoughtful. This is simply the act of focusing on ways in which we can be considerate of the feelings of others (whether we know them or not) and finding ways we can have a positive impact on their lives.

While this may not come naturally, being thoughtful requires no incredible skill. There is no skill to holding the door open for someone, but that is thoughtful. There is no skill to complimenting someone, but it is a thoughtful gesture. Being thoughtful just requires that you keep your eyes and ears open for ways to reach out and benefit others. If you focus on being thoughtful towards others, eventually it becomes a habit.

Whether or not anyone notices your acts of thoughtfulness is not important - remember you should expect nothing for your acts of altruism. All that is important is that you continue to be thoughtful. Not only will this warm your soul with good feelings about yourself, but your thoughtfulness will eventually evolve into larger deeds.

A couple simple thoughtful acts may take you from attitude to habit. Then before you know it, you go out of your way to get a referral for someone. Or, you devote an entire lunch to introducing two people even though you derive no direct benefit. Or, you might even find yourself scouring your entire network for someone who can recommend a reputable plumber - for no other reason than a neighbor needs one.

The key to successful networking is altruism - giving to others and surrendering to the notion that those gestures will find their way back to you.

To start down this path, simply ask yourself as you encounter each person in life, "How can I help them?" Then simply act upon the answers you uncover for that question. If you do, soon benefits will find their way back to you.

APPLYING THE LESSON TO LINKEDIN

Being the youngest of four children I have been accused as the "Gimme! Gimme! Gimme!" child of the family. My sisters would say it is because I am the baby and my parents gave up after the first three. I may have strived for attention as a young child, but I realized the more I begged, the less I received. Conversely I noticed the more I offered first, the more I received. This rule has held true for me into adulthood as well.

This rule also applies on LinkedIn. Those who give, get. If you accept this, it begs the question: "What are ways I can be more giving on LinkedIn?"

Here are several ideas for expressing true altruism on LinkedIn:

1. **Offer Help When It Is Least Expected:** Anytime you communicate with someone offer to help them. A simple, "Is there anything I can do to help you?" is a powerful thing.

2. **Forward Important Introductions:** If you are the "middle man" and your connection needs your help with a legitimate introduction, then pass it along. Doing this is not only an unselfish task, but it continues to build trust with that connection.

3. **Make Introductions:** This unselfish act is a great way to build trust with your connections.

4. **Provide Useful Feedback:** When you answer a question or reply to someone's status update, make sure you provide useful feedback without being like a salesperson. If you have a product that can help others, answer the question with their best interest in mind, and they will almost always check out your profile for more information.

5. **Make New-Comers Feel Welcome:** When you see a new person join LinkedIn or even a new person join in one of your groups, send them a note to better connect them to you.

6. **Make Recommendations:** Like giving a referral, a recommendation is one of the biggest compliments someone can receive. Do not wait for someone to ask you for a recommendation. You should take the initiative and write a compelling recommendation for a fellow connection.

7. **Express Gratitude:** You should always reply with a grateful message when someone offers or provides you with help. This is key in building the relationship and creating trust with your connections. You can also send random messages to people in your network telling them how grateful you are for their relationship, and how much you value their connection. These acts are always a nice gesture, and usually provoke the "boomerang effect" in return.

8. **Ask A Question:** This starts a conversation about various possibilities. Without asking, nothing will be accomplished.

9. **Start A Group:** This is a great way to become a leader for that niche, and many individuals will reach out to you for guidance. Tell others about a group: Certain contacts may be unaware of groups they would be interested in joining so lead them in the right direction.

10. **Reach Out To Help Others:** Do what you can to help others achieve their goals, and you will ultimately achieve yours along the way.

Note, these are just some ideas on how you can be altruistic on LinkedIn. You may have other thoughts and ideas. If so, great, implement what works for your personal style. Whatever you do, your efforts will come back to you.

SUCCESS STORY

Katie Felten, President, MKE LIVE

LinkedIn: www.LinkedIn.com/in/katiefelten
Website: www.mkelive.com

Katie Felten is based in Milwaukee, Wisconsin and is the president of MKE LIVE, a company she founded to provide LinkedIn seminars, LinkedIn corporate training, and other social internet media.

She is heavily involved in a variety of social networks and uses them to leverage her network and the networks of others. She is also an avid proponent of creating strategic alliances and using LinkedIn to generate more referrals.

HER STORY ... HER WORDS

I started using LinkedIn like most people do: I got an invitation from a friend, accepted it and created the start of a profile. I honestly did not do much else for about a year, other than accepting invitations. Then in June 2006, I sat down and told myself that this could be a great tool if I could just learn how to leverage it.

So I started asking people how they were using LinkedIn and looking for people who considered themselves experts, like Scott Allen and Jason Alba.

This is when I really got excited at the potential I could see for my own business. But, while I could see what it would do for me, I could also see how it benefitted others. With this enthusiasm, I started to invite people I knew to join me on LinkedIn - sort of share the wealth with them. These simple and small acts of giving began to grow my LinkedIn network immensely.

From this point, I started to share with my local friends, connections and networking groups how to best use LinkedIn. From these acts of altruism, people started to refer to me as the LinkedIn expert.

With this unofficial moniker, in the fall 2007, a friend, John Wonders, and I partnered to create a free monthly event - more giving. We called this LinkedIn LIVE, which really was a networking event to connect local people online and off. Along with asking others on LinkedIn what we should include in this program, we began sharing tips on how to best use LinkedIn at each meeting. This helped the group grow fast.

In addition to LinkedIn LIVE, we also took advantage of LinkedIn groups (creating LinkUp Milwaukee). Again, I invited more people to join in and I shared with them the power to do the same with their contacts. From this sharing and giving, the group experienced dramatic growth. It is now one of the largest in the state of Wisconsin and it continues to add over a hundred group members each month.

In early 2008, I was interested in doing more with LinkedIn. I went to a local college and offered to teach a class on all that I knew, appropriately titled LinkedIn 101. As this class was an instant success, I began the process of developing and offering more advanced classes related to LinkedIn as well as more focused classes for job seekers, recruiters and sales and marketing professionals.

LinkedIn has helped me become better networked and it has developed me as a leader and as a business person. These enhanced network opportunities, leadership skills and business acumen have served as the impetus for me to start a new business - MKE LIVE, an event and social media training company.

The most important thing to remember, which I firmly believe, is that all I have gotten from LinkedIn is a function of what I have put into it.

SUMMARY

There are no shortcuts to networking. There is, however a secret. The secret is to find as many ways as you can to help others (whether on LinkedIn or in the real world). These efforts are investments that will one day offer big returns.

BECOME ACTIVELY INVOLVED

"I am of the opinion that my life belongs to the community, and as long as I live it is my privilege to do for it whatever I can."
George Bernard Shaw

REAL WORLD NETWORKING LESSON

Louis Pasteur once said, "Chance favors the prepared mind." What Pasteur meant is that those things that most consider pure luck tend to find those that ready themselves (which is similar to and more eloquent than his less famous, "When you work seven days a week, fourteen hours a day, you get lucky.").

This same logic applies to real world networking. Restating this specifically for networking, "Opportunities accrue to the actively involved."

The foundation upon which you build a productive network is one of mutual knowing, liking and trusting. In short, you need to develop solid relationships. This, however, cannot be achieved through loose affiliations with others or just showing up from time to time.

The key syllable in the word "network" is the second one - WORK. You can never be as successful as you want by avoiding contact with other humans. You cannot achieve your networking potential hanging out in your office or cubicle and staring at your computer screen. You will not have any success at all keeping to yourself, waiting away for opportunity to find you.

Networking success requires you to get up out of your chair, leave your home or office and walk, talk and generally immerse yourself with other people. Take the time and make the effort to meet new people. Make opportunities to reconnect with those you already know. Get involved with the world around you in some way, shape or form.

This begs the question, what constitutes sufficient active involvement? To determine this, ask yourself this simple question: "If I did not show up, would I be missed?" Or more specifically, if you did not show up to work, would you be missed? If you were not at that networking event - whatever it might be - would anyone notice? If you could not make it to that meeting, would anyone know?

If after an honest, personal reflection you find the answer to any of these questions is "no" you should consider becoming more actively involved in your network. This, of course, then begs the question, "What constitutes involvement?"

There are as many levels of involvement as there are opportunities to get involved. Certainly on the one extreme, you could involve yourself by being the creator or founder of some group, club or organization. Although perhaps not as ambitious, your involvement could come in the form of serving as an officer, committee chair or board member of an existing group, club or organization.

Active involvement, however, does not necessarily require something as formal as being a founder or being in a leadership position. You can serve on committees. You can appropriately share your insights and opinions. You can even become involved by simply establishing yourself as someone willing to roll up their sleeves and get busy.

In less formal activities, you can position yourself as being actively involved as well. Start by taking the time to be around to mingle before and after the meeting - playing a sort of host to any gathering. You can also thrust yourself into the event, making meaningful contact with a collection of people and introducing them around to one another.

You can even cast yourself as being involved at work as well. You can do so by stepping up to take on that tough project or make a significant contribution to help someone else do the same. You can even become involved by engaging yourself in the social aspects of where you work, such as playing on a company team, attending outings and generally making yourself approachable.

What is so special about being involved? When you become involved - however you choose to do it - you transform yourself. When you become involved - whether at work, in the community or in any informal setting -you are no longer merely just a name on a roster or a face in the crowd. Rather when you actively involve yourself, you begin to brand yourself as a friendly and familiar face, with a warm handshake and a smile that lights up the room.

When you become actively involved, you create the perception that you are a courageous, driven and optimistic person. When you become actively involved, others get the sense that you are caring and generous. When you become actively involved, people deem you as trustworthy and reliable.

These things then combine and make it so that people cannot help but know, like and trust you - which are the building blocks for every solid professional relationship. From here it is inevitable that your network becomes more productive - and opportunities are sure to follow.

APPLYING THE LESSON TO LINKEDIN

When I used to play basketball I would make difficult shots all of the time. People would sometimes snarl at me saying, "Lucky shot Lewis... bet you can't do that again."

I did not find it lucky at all because I was in the gym for six hours a day practicing that same shot.

I never believed in luck, I believed in hard work and a passion for my sport. When others made those comments

I would always think of the quote, "Luck is what happens when preparation meets opportunity." Then I would continue preparing for those opportunities whenever I had the chance.

What does this have to do with being a successful networker on LinkedIn? Everything. You have to put the WORK in network by getting actively involved.

The things you need to do in the real world of networking to get involved include joining local groups, attending city meetings, doing community service, becoming an officer in the groups you join, and so on. The beautiful part about LinkedIn is it allows you to do those same activities in a virtual setting.

One of the most powerful features on LinkedIn is creating your own groups. A LinkedIn group is an application that can help you stay informed and keep in touch with people that share your interests.

There is great value in creating your own group. Not only does this put you as the central focus of many individuals with similar thoughts and interests, but, if done right, it makes you a very visible figure. For example, I continue to grow my personal network with quality contacts, not trying to have 50,000 plus direct connections. However, I do want to have a database of 50,000 at my fingertips for marketing purposes. And that is where LinkedIn groups come in to play.

I have created almost 15 different groups. These groups pertain to my industry, my hobbies, and my geographical location. All of these groups serve a purpose for me, and they fill a niche.

The great thing about these groups is they continue to grow on a daily basis without any work or promotion on my end. As LinkedIn continues to gain over one million members per month, more people join these groups, giving me greater access to people from all over the world.

When someone joins my group, they usually send me an e-mail with their reasons for joining, all of their contact information, and what they are currently involved with in the industry. Some even attach their resume. Here is a real example of an email I received from someone joining one of my groups:

"Hey Lewis, I've applied to join your group on LinkedIn. Currently, I'm looking to reestablish myself within the sporting industry and hope to be able to leverage the increased networking power of the group. I have attached my resume and references for further review. I hope to hear back from you at your first opportunity. Thanks in advance."

Even if they do not send me an e-mail introduction, I automatically have access to their e-mail address. Also, LinkedIn places all of the member emails on a list, and they give you the option for a one click download into an Excel® spreadsheet. Check the "Export Members" image below.

What could you do with an extra 100, 1,000, or 10,000 e-mail addresses from the top professionals in your industry? Would it be valuable to you? Absolutely!

Every time one person joins the group, everyone who is connected to that one person will see an update showing that he just joined. This entices others with similar interests to join the group as well, leaving you little work in promotion. The group grows on its own. This is a powerful tool if you take advantage of it.

Now what if there are many groups out there in your niche already? Should you create another group in the same niche? Probably not. Unless you provide a unique angle to that niche, it is wise not to create another group. Rather, you should become actively involved in an existing group.

If there are groups you would like to create but they are already out there, then introduce yourself to the group manager. Provide value to them, and offer them something to connect with you. Ask what you can do to be a manager for the group. Tell them you will provide a bi-monthly newsletter, or become involved in asking and answering questions on the discussion forum of that group. Offering more value to the group owners and offering ways to make the group more useful to them will prove to be just as beneficial to you.

Another way to become actively involved on LinkedIn is the Answers section. This section gives you the ability to ask and answer questions pertaining to any topic in any industry. People actively read these answers on a daily basis, and numerous business deals have come from individuals providing compelling information.

When you ask a question on LinkedIn, your name and profile become the focal point of the question, and the answers are the next visible thing in this section. If you ask a question, you then have the ability to rank the best answer.

These ranking points are like currency on LinkedIn. Therefore, you want to make sure you always provide helpful answers because the entire world can read them. The Answers section simply makes you more visible and involved. If your questions and answers are consistently thought-provoking and useful, then you created a positive reinforcement for your profile. The more you are recognized and seen in the Answers section or in various groups, the more people will begin to know, like and trust you.

SUCCESS STORY

Gary Unger, Author, *How To Be A Creative Genius*
(in five minutes or less)
Website: www.garyunger.com
LinkedIn: www.LinkedIn.com/in/garyunger

Gary Unger is a nationally renowned author, consultant and speaker on using LinkedIn and networking success. As a result of networking on LinkedIn.com, his book sold out at Amazon.com (twice), Borders and Barnes & Noble during the launch of the book.

Additionally, through networking on LinkedIn, he has been interviewed across the world regarding both his book and his networking on LinkedIn. Also, he has received numerous requests to write about his success for books, magazines and blogs.

LinkedIn has served as a good connection for people to find him and invite him to speak at their events. Along with these networking successes, a television show is in production and should be airing in early 2009. Currently he is talking with other broadcast networks and producers about another series of television shows.

HIS STORY ... HIS WORDS

When I first started on LinkedIn I did not get much of a return. This began to change once I involved myself in the LinkedIn community.

My involvement started with me simply answering questions that others had posted. At first I was afraid of "giving away the store" with my advice or perspective on a question posed by other members. But then it hit me: While I may be losing a possible consulting gig with the questioner, there are others who are reading my reply that may like my take on business, and request that I consult with them.

My hunch was right. After I started freely answering questions with honest answers or the hint of a return for my advice, I started getting the inquiries for my business services.

I took the advice of my publisher who suggested that I soft sell my book when I give advice. Meaning I would not always try to make a sale, instead I would simply provide the opportunity for someone to come look at my book or website. It worked; my site started getting direct hits from LinkedIn.

When a question I was answering did call for a direct sell of my book, I took those opportunities as well. It is a balancing act at times to do a hard sell or a soft sell in an answer, but the majority of my selling came down to soft selling.

Because I saw in other people's answers and questions a constant hard sell, I decided the stigma of "that guy" was not worth gaining a few immediate book purchases.

One of the best ways for me to connect with others when I had no other way of connecting to was to post questions. These were honest questions about business, LinkedIn itself, and my own hobbies and interests. From this, suddenly, I had people connecting with me who answered a question or saw the question and invited me into their network.

Then again at the advice of my publisher I further involved myself by joining groups. In addition, I created my own and used them to involve myself in LinkedIn. For example, I created The Creative Fortune Cookie Group. From this I would e-mail group members an interesting quote that would inspire thinking and creativity. The concept was simple. Each week, I would e-mail members a one or two sentence quote that would be controversial, or something very uncommon. There were no big graphics or sales pitches, just the quote and lots of space before my e-mail signature, which contained a link to my profile and the book. Again, there was no hard selling - just the opportunity.

Through this group I was able to connect with people who are not "networkers" but had interest in getting inspirational e-mails. Starting my own group enabled me to contact people who aren't active networkers but have similar interests, thus expanding my network.

I encourage active participation on LinkedIn in the form of asking questions, answering questions, joining groups and starting groups. Networking is not about being behind the scenes and navigating.

It is about knocking on doors and seeing which doors open. Some doors open later than others, but eventually they still open.

SUMMARY

You cannot expect to grow your business by sitting in your office or home all day. You have to get out there...attend different events...be a resource for others...stay connected with your colleagues, clients, and potential customers. The same is true on LinkedIn. You cannot just set up a profile and wait for people to come to you. You must reach out to the LinkedIn community and become actively involved.

LinkedWorking

PLAY THE KEVIN BACON GAME

"The real death of America will come when everyone is alike."
James T. Ellison

REAL WORLD NETWORKING LESSON

A key to networking success is having a diverse group of contacts. You are further ahead having a connection with 100 people, each of who is from a different organization, than knowing 1,000 people from one organization.

As many of the people in the one organization know one another (or know someone who knows someone else), much of the network of the person with the 1,000 connections is redundant. The person connected to only 100 people, however, has little redundancy as he or she knows people from presumably various industries and parts of the country.

An interesting way of demonstrating the validity of this point is, at least indirectly, through the Kevin Bacon Game. People play this informal game at parties or around the water coolers of corporate America. The object is to link any actor to the actor Kevin Bacon through the movies in which they have appeared.

For example, if someone gives another in the game, the name Mary Pickford, the person receiving the name would have to link her to Kevin Bacon in less than six steps. According to what I have been able to determine, you can actually do this in three. Here goes ... Mary Pickford was in "Screen Snapshots" with Clark Gable ... Step One ... Then Clark Gable was in "Combat America" with Tony Romano ... Step Two ... Finally, Tony Romano, 35 years later, was in "Starting Over" with Kevin Bacon. Step Three.

While for many the Kevin Bacon Game offers nothing but pure amusement, for others it provides the inspiration for scientific exploration.

This was certainly true for Brett Tjaden and Glenn Wasson, two students at the University of Virginia who were each working towards their graduate degrees in computer science. In 1996, the pair created a website called the Oracle of Kevin Bacon - http://oracleofbacon.org/. Using the Internet Movie Database, this website allowed anyone to determine quickly how many steps any actor is from Kevin Bacon.

In addition to developing the Oracle of Kevin Bacon, these computer scientists developed a program that allowed them to use the Internet Movie Database to determine that Kevin Bacon was on average 2.8312 steps from any actor. Thus, someone could link Kevin Bacon to the majority of actors listed on the Internet Movie Database in less than three steps on average. Obviously, this figure changes with the release of each movie, as the activities of actors increases the connectivity of Kevin Bacon.

Using this program, these computer scientists then did this same analysis for every actor in the Internet Movie Database. They determined the average number of steps any actor is from any other actor in the Internet Movie Database. Armed with these results, they rank ordered the actors, determining at the time that Kevin Bacon placed 668th of all actors.

Among the top 50 were names such as Martin Sheen, Gene Hackman, and Donald Sutherland. Interestingly enough, this analysis ranked actor Burgess Meredith, who appeared in 114 films, in the top 20. This analysis, however, also ranked John Wayne at 160th on the list, even though he appeared in 183 films - almost 70 more films than Burgess Meredith did.

This difference begs the question: Why is John Wayne ranked so much lower than Burgess Meredith (when he appeared in approximately 60% more movies)? The answer is not in the number of movies each appeared in, but rather in the types of movies in which they appeared.

John Wayne appeared in lots of films, but they were all the same sort of film - westerns and war movies. Some of these include *Bardelays The Magnificent* (1926), *Texas Cyclone* (1932), *The Sands of Iwo Jima* (1949), *The Green Berets* (1968), and *Rooster Cogburn* (1975). In each of these films, John Wayne worked with one particular cross-section of actors. In fact, it is difficult to discern between some John Wayne films as he appears on screen with the same people in similar roles.

Burgess Meredith, on the other hand, appeared in a wide variety of movies: 42 dramas (including *Of Mice and Men* (1939) and *Rocky* (1976)) ... 22 comedies ... eight adventures ... seven action ... five documentaries, science fiction, horror and western ... four thrillers and crime movies ... two children, romance and mysteries ... a musical and an animated film. By being involved with a broad section of project types, Burgess Meredith overall worked with a very diverse group of actors. This makes him highly connected within the Internet Movie Database.

In this disparity is support for my initial premise in this chapter - a key to networking success is having a diverse group of contacts. Examine your network. Does your network resemble the career of John Wayne? Do you go to work? Play softball or watch the big game with the people with whom you work? Do you consume your social calendar with things involving your co-workers? If the answer is yes, you probably feel as if your network is stagnant.

On the other hand, does your network look like Burgess Meredith's career? Are you involved with youth sports, the PTA and the local garden club? Do you have an active membership in a trade association? Are the people you socialize with people with whom you have no other real contact? If so, you are probably wonderfully overwhelmed with the variety of contacts you have and the various benefits they bring to you.

Whether your network resembles Burgess Meredith's career, John Wayne's or somewhere in between, you now know that a key to networking success is having a diverse group of contacts.

APPLYING THE LESSON TO LINKEDIN

During my first two years in high school I remember only hanging out with the "athlete" crowd, and I was either too cool or too afraid to disperse myself in other groups. As I started to become more mature, older friends graduated, and my taste for new hobbies changed, I began to spend time with a wide variety of classmates.

Sure, I was considered a "jock" but there were many other things that inspired me, which I began to take on. I joined the choir, was a lead in our schools musical, took tap dancing class, learned to play the guitar, and traveled the country. By doing so I began to appreciate and spend time with a diverse number of students. I created some lasting relationships, met a wide variety of influential individuals, and have been able to create exciting opportunities from these interactions.

When I first joined LinkedIn, I started off by only connecting with former classmates, and people from my hometown. This is not a bad thing, but my network would only reach as far as the alumni from my school, and the people of Columbus, Ohio. When I began to update my profile on LinkedIn I knew that the diversification principles in real life might work just as well.

So how should you diversify on LinkedIn? Connect yourself with people from a number of "cliques" that interest you. If you are a business professional and you love music, theater and novels then send an invitation to musicians, actors, and writers who seem interesting to you. Create a conversation with these people and tell them why you find them interesting, why you are passionate about their genre and if there is anything you can do to help their career. Maybe you can connect them to someone in your business world that will help to boost their career, and maybe, eventually, they can even use your services.

I recommend that you join a variety of total groups as well. Currently I am in several groups, all which pertain to some interest of mine. I am in a public speaking group, a group for inventors, bloggers, medical professionals, innovation, entrepreneurs, financial success, marketing, city networking groups, and a number of sports and athlete related groups.

Here are some suggestions for expanding your network into a variety of "cliques":

1. **Group Diversification:** Type in key phrases in the group directory that are of interest to you. There is a group for nearly every interest, and if there is not, create the group yourself and become the LinkedIn jetsetter.

2. **People Watch:** Once you join a group, take some time to browse through profiles, and reach out to those who you find interesting.

3. **Group Introductions:** The best way to get accepted in a real world clique is becoming friends with the leader. This is also true on LinkedIn. Group moderators are the leaders of every group. Connect with these individuals by sending them a message explaining the passion you share for their niche.

4. **Offer Group Assistance:** Ask group founders if there is any way you can help. Tell them that you will create a Yahoo or Google group/forum so members may share information better. This can be an easy way of gaining acceptance from the rest of the members.

SUCCESS STORY

Adam J. Kovitz, CEO, Founder and Publisher,
The National Networker

Website: www.TheNationalNetworker.com
LinkedIn: www.LinkedIn.com/in/ajkovitz

Adam J. Kovitz is one of the world's recognized thought-leaders on relationship networking, the relationship economy and relationship capital.

He is the CEO, founder and publisher of *The National Networker,* a free online magazine that serves as a positively-charged "Consumer Reports of Networking".

Adam started the publication with just 900 readers in February 2005 as a means to inform the public, which was hungry for meaningful networking experiences, yet did not have the time (nor money) to find the right opportunities. This insight, combined with unique content, launched *The National Networker (TNNW)* to national, then international recognition.

In addition to writing his own monthly column in the "pages" of TNNW, he is also a contributing author to *The Emergence of the Relationship Economy.* He has been a featured speaker for numerous organizations and has been interviewed on several podcasts and radio shows. Adam also serves on the advisory board for several networking organizations and is the co-founder and former executive director of the Relationship Networking Industry Association.

HIS STORY ... HIS WORDS

I grew up in the small, suburban, yet historic Hightstown, New Jersey, after our family moved there from Brooklyn. This was a contributing factor to what I consider a "small-town" mentality. For the first 35 years of my life I lived in the same town, where I settled down after college and started my family.

That, however, changed shortly after I discovered a passion for networking. As a Director with Business Network International (BNI), I studied the world of offline networking. Then in 2004, I discovered the brave new world of online networking.

It was a wondrous place and, while very foreign to me, it was also welcoming. I had a restlessness to grow outside of my own comfort zone because I had a vision of something much larger than myself...the worlds first "Consumer Reports of Networking", called *The National Networker* (or "TNNW" for short). To realize this, I had to become much larger in scope and influence than where I was. In short, I needed writers from other parts of the country and eventually, the world. This was a challenge considering that my "extensive network" was dug deep in New Jersey, especially Mercer County where I grew up.

Initially, I had some success doing Internet searches with an immediate follow-up of cold calls. I was on my way, yet slowly. At the time, I was not taking online networking too seriously, as it seemed "clunky" and "confusing" to me.

Sometime after my first year of TNNW, I decided to sit down and figure out LinkedIn just to see if it would accelerate my effort. On a whim, I decided to fill out my profile a bit more than I had, as well as include my vision for TNNW. Then I figured I would set about inviting a few strangers to join my network. But who?

One of the first was Mike O'Neil. There was something about his profile that seemed of interest to me. He had his own networking organization in Denver, Colorado - Integrated Alliances. Through Integrated Alliances he taught other people how to network using LinkedIn. I was not sure if he would like me or reject me, but with a bit of courage I pressed the send button. Within an hour or so, he became my first random connection on LinkedIn and sent me a message that he wanted to write for TNNW!

As I got to know Mike, he helped me perfect my profile and even gave me a strategy for expanding my network quickly, which I did. He also told me about a great group run by Vincent Wright, called "My LinkedIn Power Forum", which was a Yahoo group of dedicated LinkedIn power users and LinkedIn staff. I joined with that group and over time met great people like Jay Deragon, Scott Allen and Margaret Orem (all with whom I wrote the book, The Emergence of the Relationship Economy), Jason Alba (before his fame with JibberJobber and his book *I'm on LinkedIn, Now What?*), Terry Bean, Chris Kauza, Andy Lopata, Victor Cattermole and a host of others.

The interesting thing is that these contacts came from all walks of life. There are computer types, entrepreneurs, authors and sales people. It is this diversity that gives my network strength. As you peruse the contacts page of TNNW's website, half of my nearly 40 writers are connections from LinkedIn.

Today, TNNW has a worldwide audience and a presence across the U.S. as well as Canada, the UK and Asia Pacific. And while my words may come to a close, the story is far from over. Every new week brings more invitations to connect on LinkedIn as well as more insight from Vincent Wright's forum.

And if you are not already within three degrees of Kevin Bacon, connect with me on LinkedIn and you will be! How? Kevin once attended the annual performance of the Nutcracker at the Academy of Music in Philadelphia. My nephew (who now dances for the New York Ballet) was the prince in the production and got to meet and sit with Kevin.

Our world continues to get smaller every day...enjoy the ride.

SUMMARY

Always be sure to broaden your horizons as it relates to whom you associate. Yes, it is important to be a well-known and respected professional in your niche area of interest, but this will only take you so far. In the real world and on LinkedIn, move out of your own "clique" and connect with individuals and groups that pertain to anything you are interested in, and continue to be a useful resource for all of those with whom you connect.

LinkedWorking

HARNESS THE POWER OF RECONNECTION

"Each contact with a human being is so rare,
so precious, one should preserve it."
Anais Nin

REAL WORLD NETWORKING LESSON

Everyone has networking opportunity for you. I have made that abundantly clear. I am the first to admit, however, that networking success involves a multi-faceted approach.

While being open to literally everyone you encounter is a powerful concept, it can be somewhat generally focused more on habits and attitudes than specific activities. After all, there are lots of people out there - approximately six-point-five billion in the world and growing. While you will never encounter most of these, many you will only meet once. Therefore, it is important to focus on networking strategies that are action oriented and closer to home.

When you think of networking, what do you think of? You think of meeting new people, right? This is by no means an innovative revelation. It is your hope then, that these new people will need what you have to offer. Or at the very least, you are certainly hopeful that these new people will introduce you to still more new people. Sooner or later, somebody will need what you have to offer.

So when you say, "I am going to do some networking" you are in essence saying, "I am trying to meet someone new." There is nothing inherently flawed with this logic. Most articles and books on the topic of networking focus almost exclusively on the art or science of meeting these new people and making them productive feeders of business referrals and opportunities for the reader.

While there is nothing wrong with this logic, it is shortsighted. What about your accountant? What about your high school friend or college roommate? What about the folks at the gym? Focusing exclusively on making new contacts ignores individuals you already know -- a powerful and vital segment of your network. The truth of the matter is that, whether you are 19, 90 or in between, you already know more people than you will meet in the next year - maybe even the next two or three.

What is so special about people you already know? Simple. If you already know them, then they presumably know you. And if they know you, then it is not too much of a stretch to assume that they also like you and trust you. It is this "know, like and trust" that is the very foundation upon which a productive networking relationship is built. Therefore, reconnecting with people we already know can be an effective networking strategy. It can jump start a sputtering network or send a productive network into overdrive.

Consider Theodore Geisel, better known by his pseudonym Dr. Seuss. In the summer of 1936, Seuss decided to get serious about his writing career. Seuss had an interest in doing some lighthearted writing for children, an interest that dated back to his days on the staff of a humor magazine at Dartmouth College.

In short order, Seuss easily completed his first book, *And To Think That I Saw It On Mulberry Street*. Getting it published was a different matter, however.

Seuss was told that his story was too different, as it was not like the Dick and Jane stories for children of the time. He was told that the verses were too difficult for children to read. And most troublesome of all, he was told that his story did not have any sort of moral to help children become better citizens. In all, during the winter of 1936-37, he got 27 rejections.

Upon receiving word of his 27th rejection, Seuss headed home to stage a ceremonial burning of the now tattered manuscript. As he grimly walked along Madison Avenue, he met up with an old friend from Dartmouth, Mike McClintock.

Seuss shared his woes. McClintock simply smiled, as three hours earlier he had become juvenile editor of Vanguard Press. Within 30 minutes, he got Vanguard Press to commit to publish Seuss' work, which launched the Dr. Seuss legend. In short, it was a simple, almost chance, reconnection with an old friend that launched him into becoming one of the most beloved children's authors of the twentieth century.

There is certainly enormous power in reconnecting with those you already know. This, however, almost begs the question: What is the best way to reconnect? After all, you cannot rely on the luck that Dr. Seuss experienced.

Donna Fisher, in her book *People Power*, has some straightforward advice: Simply call. Labeling this a "Reconnection Call", Fisher indicates that it is made for the purpose of "reestablishing a relationship."

Once you have the person on the line, simply acknowledge that it has been a long time, and then express an interest in catching up. Although it may feel awkward at first, remember your old friend is being reconnected too. Therefore, your call will be a welcome benefit to him or her as well.

And to think, people told Seuss that *Mulberry Street* had no sort of moral to help us become better citizens.

APPLYING THE LESSON TO LINKEDIN

LinkedIn is the best way to reconnect with the people you already know. If you have not spoken to someone in years, or if you would like to build a better relationship with those you already know, LinkedIn gives you the opportunity to connect.

Who can you reconnect with?

- **Connect with Colleagues:** There is no better way to build your connections than by starting with the people you currently work with or have worked with in the past. The majority of your colleagues are most likely already on LinkedIn, giving you the option to expand your network. LinkedIn makes it easy to connect with everyone from your current company or those in the past.

- **Connect with Classmates:** Why go to your 20-year reunion when you can have a virtual reunion online? You can view classmates from your graduation year, or any year you attended school. You may be surprised who you see, but if you had any connection with them in school, you will want to reconnect here as well. You never know how the relationship will be beneficial, and you don't want to lose out on any opportunities.

How do you reconnect with others?

- **Invite Contacts:** LinkedIn allows you to invite your contacts to join your personal network by sending them a personal reconnect. You should have fun with this and write something interesting to those relationships that are not as strong. For example: "Hey Chris, I know we have not spoken in a while but I thought it would be fun to connect with you in cyberspace. Let's grab some coffee in the near future. I would love to catch up with you face to face as well."

- **Import Contacts:** LinkedIn also gives you the ability to easily upload all of your current contacts with the click of a button. Hotmail, Yahoo, Gmail, AOL, and Outlook are easily imported directly into LinkedIn (see the image below). You can see who already has a profile on LinkedIn, and connect with them first. Then you can send personal invitations to those who you think would benefit from having a profile.

SUCCESS STORY

Matthew Guehl, Recruiter, The Gammill Group and Founder, LinkedColumbus

LinkedIn: www.LinkedIn.com/in/mattguehl
Website: www.gammilgroup.com

Matt Guehl is an executive recruiter with the Gammill Group in Columbus, Ohio. Matt specializes in executive-level talent acquisition within the health care industry on a national level.

He is the founder of LinkedColumbus, a LinkedIn group for professionals who are either located in the Greater Columbus, Ohio area or who have a personal or professional connection to the area. The mission of LinkedColumbus is to build and improve relationships which will ultimately benefit Columbus as a whole.

HIS STORY ... HIS WORDS

Late in the year of 2007 I was fumbling my way around LinkedIn and noticed a Group Directory. I began to look into this unknown area of LinkedIn and realized that I could create a dynamic informal subset of Columbus, Ohio professionals that wanted to have direct contact with each other.

From this epiphany, I created a group called LinkedColumbus and sent an e-mail to about 20 of my friends and clients in Columbus, asking them to join this group, allowing us to network with others who had a vested interest in Columbus. I asked them to spread the word to anyone they felt would provide value to the group.

I figured that each person I knew would know at least two others that utilize LinkedIn, or would recommend it to capitalize on the value of the Columbus group.

As trust and credibility were already established amongst those they were inviting and, because the recommendation came from an established relationship, I assumed that most invitations would be accepted. I was correct.

It was at that point the group was set in motion and it has not let up since. During the first few weeks the group grew at a steady rate of about 10 requests per week. I anticipated the group would be approximately 500 members within the first six months.

I underestimated the power of networking, however. Within five months, the group grew to well over 1,000 members. With this base of group membership, I decided it was time to schedule the groups first in-person networking event - May 15th, 2008.

The event was an informal environment for professionals to build new friendships and business relationships. We had a great turnout, with over 250 members attending.

Since that initial event, word has continued to spread, mainly through group members reconnecting with those they already knew in Columbus who were on LinkedIn. As a result, the group is now 3,500 members and still growing. Not only has the LinkedColumbus group expanded my network, it has reconnected me with past colleagues and friends that would have otherwise remained in the shadows.

I truly believe the success of this group is due to the diversity of the members, which is based on the simple desire to be connected to other Columbus professionals.

Everyone in the group now has new connections with over 3,500 people who share a common interest which opens up endless possibilities to extend their network. By finding a common interest, with someone you already know and, by proactively being a center of influence, you can quickly become acquainted with many others. The key is for you to make it happen. Do not wait for them to find you.

SUMMARY

When you are networking, the temptation is to continually reach out to total strangers. While there is merit in meeting new people, there is incredible power in reconnecting with those you already know.

LinkedWorking

TAKE CONSISTENT ACTION

"I don't wait for moods.
You accomplish nothing if you do that.
Your mind must know it has got to get down to work."
Pearl S. Buck

REAL WORLD NETWORKING LESSON

If you want to be healthy, you need to undertake certain activities. It does not just happen. You need to eat right, exercise and get plenty of sleep. Without these activities, chances are that your health will suffer.

The same is true if you want a successful network - you need to undertake certain activities. You need to meet new people, reconnect with those you know and do all those things that help create and maintain relationships. It does not just happen.

With being healthy, you cannot expect it to happen if you engage in the required activities occasionally and then ignore them the rest of the time. The same is true of networking. You must undertake the activities consistently.

This does not mean that you need to pour yourself into networking activities every minute of every day. But by the same token, you cannot engage in a single networking activity and expect that it alone will create networking success.

Far too often, people approach their networking like they do their health. They lead their life with little focus on their health, becoming unfit, round and soft in the process. Or in networking terms, they avoid growing their contact base and allow their current relationships to stagnate.

Then something happens. From a health perspective, it may be the trip of a lifetime, a wedding or that high school reunion. From a networking perspective, it might be a need to find a new job or to obtain critical information to land that key account.

In either respect, what follows is a massive amount of activity, focused on undoing the neglectful past. For health, that might mean crash diets, extreme exercise routines or even medical procedures. For networking, they embark upon a whirlwind of activities (telephone calls, letter campaigns and face-to-face meetings), all attempting to undo months (or even years) of neglect in a few short weeks.

Although these activities represent a massive effort over a short duration, the reality is that these catch-up efforts pale in comparison to moderate consistent action over an extended period. As such, there is a much greater return on consistent action - in both networking and health endeavors.

To set yourself on the path of consistent action, start by establishing certain goals you want to achieve through your networking efforts. How many new people do you want to meet in a given period? How often do you want to connect with those you already know? How much and what type of value do you want to give to those you know?

Once you have established goals, plan out the required activities for meeting your goals. For example, if your goals have a heavy focus on meeting new people, then your consistent actions need to be centered on activities that will bring you in front of those you do not know. Remember, whether you set out this regime of activities formally or informally, each one should serve to drive the betterment of your network.

Finally, you need to take action. As with anything, a goal and a plan to achieve it is nothing without activity to see it through. No matter what your goals are, and no matter what your plans are to achieve those goals, the key is consistent, moderate action - and not the occasional massive type.

APPLYING THE LESSON TO LINKEDIN

"Consistent, moderate action" is important in order to build and maintain a healthy network on LinkedIn. Thus, it is important to create balance while on LinkedIn, and not try to overdo it. To achieve this balance, I recommend a simple, three-step system: Goal, Plan, and Action.

Step 1: Goal.

>   The first step to anything in LinkedIn is to develop a goal. What specifically do you want to achieve on LinkedIn in a specific time frame? You should write it out exactly. For example: "I want to become a leading expert in the sports industry, promote my products, showcase my networking expertise, receive six speaking engagements this year, improve my personal brand, and add value for everyone with whom I come in contact."

Step 2: Plan.

>   After setting a goal, develop a plan in writing that will get you there. Below is a sample list for LinkedIn.
>
>   • Spend up to 60 minutes a day on LinkedIn -- 30 in the morning or evening and 30 minutes in the early afternoon, as these are the times when most users are active on LinkedIn.
>
>   • Invite five important/influential/interesting people to my network each week.
>
>   • E-mail and ask a compelling question to three people I want to know better.
>
>   • Make a telephone call to at least two people per week (first sending a respectful e-mail to see if they would be open to the conversation).

- Update my status every two days to keep others informed.

- Develop one question per week and send it to at least 50 qualified people for response.

- Answer three questions per week on subjects in which I want to be recognized.

- Recommend one person per week.

- Every week, respond to five interesting individuals who join one of my groups.

- Reply to all personalized messages within 48 hours.

STEP 3: ACTION.

A goal and plan are useless without action, making this the most important step in the process. To ensure action, print copies of your plan and put them in various locations where you will see them, especially next to your computer.

By printing your goals and plan and having them around for you to see, you will keep yourself focused. In addition, take time every day to review your goals, and the plan you need to execute and achieve them. While doing so, check items off the list when completed. At the end of every week, look back at all the things you have done. You will be amazed at how many interesting people you will meet, and what kind of opportunities will unfold by following this process.

SUCCESS STORY

Jason Alba, CEO, JibberJobber.com

Author: *I'm on LinkedIn -- Now What???*
LinkedIn: www.LinkedIn.com/in/jasonalba
Website: www.jasonalba.com

Jason Alba is a nationally renowned expert on LinkedIn, as well as the author of the acclaimed book, *I'm On LinkedIn, Now What???* In addition, he is the founder of JibberJobber. com, a personal job search tool he designed after being frustrated with his own job search.

JibberJobber.com helps professionals manage career and job search activities the same way a salesperson manages prospects and customer data.

HIS STORY ... HIS WORDS

When I started using LinkedIn to market my business, I knew that the status quo strategy was not going to be of any benefit to me. You know: post a profile, wait for people to connect to me and hope for the best.

I wanted to get my name, brand and services in front of LinkedIn's millions of users. I knew I'd have to work to become known, and optimize the relationships I was forming on LinkedIn. One thing that stood out as an opportunity to increase my brand visibility was answering questions. I started answering questions that weren't self-promotional, but rather would remind people of what my interests were.

I also realized that answering questions posted on LinkedIn would be a great way to show my expertise, meet new people, and develop relationships. This has been great.

In addition, I regularly export my contacts and put them into my JibberJobber database so I can manage the relationship with them. From here, I'll add people to my personal newsletter so my contacts know what I'm up to, and how they can help me.

I have a statement on my LinkedIn profile summary that says, "I will add you to my newsletter if you choose to connect with me." I can always tell who has read my profile by their invitation as they'll say, "I'd love to get your newsletter." I feel strongly about nurturing relationships, not just adding people to increase your numbers, and sending out newsletters is my way of keeping in touch with each of my contacts in a professional way on a regular basis.

Any time you can go deeper than having a profile and accepting connections, when you can put your brand out there and get to know your contacts better (and let them get to know you), you will get more value out of LinkedIn.

SUMMARY

The greatest of achievements - The Great Wall of China, Microsoft or the National Football League (just to name a few) - did not just occur. They were built over time with consistent, moderate action. The same is true of your networking, whether on LinkedIn or in the real world.

BE CONCISE, COMPELLING
AND VALUE-DRIVEN

"Nobody counts the number of ads you run; they just remember
the impression you make."
William Bernbach

REAL WORLD NETWORKING LESSON

They say, "You only have one chance to make a first impression." While that is true, you also only have a limited time in which to do it.

Whether you are connecting with someone for the first time, the tenth time or somewhere in between, you have a finite time in which to get your message across. People are busy. For the most part they do not have time to be consumed with the details of every nuance of your business, product or life.

Consider your resume. You limit your resume to one or two pages, even though you could yammer on and on about all your accomplishments and achievements. Whatever the objective of your resume, you have only a small window of opportunity to capture the attention of the reviewer. If you do not, that person is on to the next one - in essence, casting you aside.

The same logic applies to other mediums of communication. Your website, company brochure or other collateral pieces must be succinct and to the point. People want to know right away who you are and what you are about.

This does not preclude you from having more information available. It may be in the form of text further into the brochure, or other pages on the website. Nevertheless, your first impression needs to be concise, compelling and value-driven.

The same is true of one-on-one networking encounters. The same "concise, compelling and value-driven" rules apply. And these rules continue to apply unless and until you and the other person are so completely comfortable with each other that the conversation can meander through a litany of polite pleasantries, such as "How are the kids?" At which point, the relationship graduates to one more social in nature.

The goal of any networking encounter is to convey a short message that says enough to get them wanting more. You do not have much more than 30 seconds to a minute to accomplish this. This is the approximate time you might spend riding an elevator, hence many use the term "elevator speech" to describe this introductory portion of a conversation.

Note that there is no magic formula for an elevator speech. It should, however, have a minimum of three important elements.

1. **Who You Are:** Somewhere in that initial time frame of conversation, you need to succinctly establish who you are. For example, an elevator speech for me might include:

    "I am Frank Agin, President of AmSpirit Business Connections."

2. **What You Do:** In addition to who you are, you need to provide an overview of what you do. Following the above example, I might state the following:

    "AmSpirit Business Connections empowers its members to become more successful through networking. Membership consists of entrepreneurs, sales representatives and professionals. These members then participate in a weekly structured meeting format designed to help them generate referrals from other members."

3. **Establish Credibility:** Much of the networking process is about creating and maintaining a relationship. In other words, you are building the critical elements of "know, like and trust." You generally do this through other people's first hand experience with you. Without that first hand experience, however, you can start to build these elements with a short statement that serves to establish credibility. Continuing on with the example from above, I might state:

   "AmSpirit Business Connections has dozens of Chapters throughout the United States with hundreds of members - many of whom have been participating in the organization for well over 10 years."

Again, it is important to note that there is no single "correct" formula for creating a concise, compelling and value-driven elevator speech for yourself. There are lots of different approaches to wrapping the above three basic ideas into one. A discussion of all those approaches is beyond the scope of this book.

Whatever approach you choose to aid you in being concise, compelling and value-driven, it is important to remember that you ought to develop a variety of elevator speeches for yourself. For example, a real estate agent might have an elevator speech for situations in which they are connecting with a potential home seller, and then an entirely different one for when they are talking with a potential home buyer.

Over the years, I have found it helpful to actually write out my elevator speeches. Not only does this allow you to create an inventory, but also provides you with something you can review from time to time as a means of practicing. After all, the more time you spend thinking through your elevator speech, the more it becomes second nature.

APPLYING THE LESSON TO LINKEDIN

First impressions mean everything, especially on LinkedIn. You have about 30 seconds to give your elevator pitch to someone in the 'real world'. Online, however, you have about three seconds at most. People will read your name and your headline, and it if is not somehow concise, compelling, and value-driven, they are on to the next one.

This is why it is important to spend some time creating an interesting headline and profile. When someone searches your name on Google, your LinkedIn profile is usually the first thing that appears.

You don't write in a boring manner on your resume. Instead, you write about all of the amazing things you have done in your work experience, and then some. So take that same approach to your LinkedIn profile and make it just as compelling as your resume.

Now it is possible to take this too far and in my opinion some people go over the top. When you go over the top, it is almost always because you are lacking something. People see through this facade and tend to gravitate away from you. Here is an example of what not to write:

Joe Schmo [LION] (Open Networker)
Joeschmo@shmuck.com[TopLinked]

OPEN NETWORKER (LION) - TOP LINKED, 1100+ connections, Internet Marketing-Executive ► Social-Media-Expert► SEM ► SEO ► PPA► PPC ► Web 2.0 ► New Media Guru and Guerilla Social Networking King!

Shmuckville Area, Loserland

This is too much. People do not need to see that you are a "LION" or a "TopLinked" next to your name. You can have this in your headline if you prefer to attract other open networkers, but you do not need to make it stand out over everything else.

Now let's look at a profile that will show how you can still have the flash, but in a more value driven way. Stan Relihan from Sydney, Australia is one of LinkedIn's top 50 connected users. He is the CEO at Expert Executive Search, a company that prides itself on finding the best employees for companies. He prides himself on being one of the most connected individuals in his profession, and LinkedIn has helped this tremendously. Here is Stan's headline:

Stan's headline is well done. He gives his name and does so without extra LinkedIn add-ons. He then starts off by saying something compelling and value-driven: "Asia-Pacific's Most-Connected Headhunter". He then tells us how many people he is connected with on LinkedIn to back it up, 20,000+.

Stan then writes that he is a public speaker and networker. This means he is willing to talk, provide guidance, offer help, connect you with someone else, and be a useful resource. He catches your attention in about three seconds and gives you the impression that he is someone with whom you want to connect. This is one reason why nearly 100 people send him an invitation to connect every day.

I do not get nearly as many people requesting to connect as Stan. I do, however, receive a dozen or so quality contacts every week that are valuable to me. My headline is simple, but I attract the people I want to attract:

People who usually connect with me are athletes, professionals in the sports business, other entrepreneurs or product developers. If you are an IT professional, my headline may not interest you. If you are in my industry, however, you may be interested in connecting and learning more.

Whether you are working to be a leader in your industry, or you would like 100 people to invite you to connect daily, then you need to be concise, compelling, and value-driven in your entire profile, not just your headline. The headline is what brings people in, but it will only take you so far.

You need to make sure that every section of your profile is concise, compelling, and full of rich value. Go through my checklist to make sure each section has met these criteria, and you will begin to see vast improvements in your network.

THE LINKEDWORKING CHECKLIST

Profile Completeness

- ☐ Name
- ☐ Headline
- ☐ Location
- ☐ Personal Picture

Work Experience

- ☐ Current Work
- ☐ Relevant Previous Experience
(Add brief content for each position)

Education

- ☐ List All Colleges
Promote groups, societies, activities, and other achievements

Industry Relevance

- ☐ Submit industry you want to be found in
- ☐ List all relevant personal websites

Profile URL

- ☐ Create personal branding URL- either your name,company, or one or two word tag line summary
- ☐ Write compelling content on what you do and how you can help others-write for the people who you want to find your profile

Specialties:

- ☐ Include one or two word descriptions from summary
- ☐ Write for your industry

Recommendations:

- ☐ At least six recommendations for reputable branding

Interests:

- ☐ Including interests give you more personality

Groups and Associations:

- ☐ Provide all relevant groups or clubs of which you are a member in the real world, and add the ones on LinkedIn that are important to you.

Group Visibility:

- ☐ Make visible the groups you want others to see, and change visibility if you don't want the public to see your group membership

Honors and Awards:

- ☐ Display awards and achievements to build credibility with industry members

Contact Settings:

- ☐ Add the e-mail address at which you want to receive messages
- ☐ Add a phone number if you want people to call you
- ☐ Add all contact opportunities that interest you

Groups:

- ☐ Join groups in your industry, city, state, university, and in your other interests
- ☐ Create a group of your specialty if one is not available

Contacts:

- ☐ Send invite requests from all email addresses (such as Outlook, Gmail, AOL, YAHOO!, Hotmail) to all connections already members of LinkedIn.
- ☐ Invite a select few who could benefit the most by joining
- ☐ Connect with colleagues from previous and past work experiences
- ☐ Connect with classmates from your school

SUCCESS STORY

Nathan C. Kievman, Strategic Alliance and Joint Venture Specialist

LinkedIn: www.LinkedIn.com/in/nkievman
Website: www.businesssuccessunlimited.com

Nathan Kievman is a strategic alliance and joint venture specialist, business growth consultant and marketing strategist. His primary emphasis is helping small to medium sized businesses create exponential growth for their company. In order to bring practical value to his clients, he interacts with some of the biggest names in marketing and business.

Having interviewed a self-made billionaire, one of the world's most renowned business consultants, as well as top-level executives and business owners throughout the country, Nathan takes great honor in being able to provide his visitors with his conversations on business success secrets for free.

HIS STORY ... HIS WORDS

I ask a lot of questions on the LinkedIn discussion boards. You can tell a lot about someone's approach from the responses you get. For me to find success in business I had to find a way to be concise, compelling and value driven at all times.

I have launched an interview series, a consultation practice, landed contracts worth hundreds of thousands of dollars and created entire advisory boards based on this insightful topic, which is to be concise, compelling and value driven.

Being concise is the only way I have been able to get in front of the biggest names in business for my interview series. But by itself, being concise means nothing if it is not also compelling. You must be compelling to capture the attention of a fast moving and focused individual. To be compelling, however, one must be value driven. Being value driven is hands down the most important thing for any business owner. Being value driven is not as basic or easy as many people believe.

For example, look at a discussion board on LinkedIn and see how many people are actually value-driven? Most of them are self-driven - either subtly or blatantly looking for something they hope to achieve for themselves. However, if you ask insightful questions that are thought-provoking, you end up getting better results. Trust me, I have experienced this success through LinkedIn firsthand.

I have used LinkedIn to create traffic for my website, build an advisory board, use it as a place to get answers to complex business questions, and much more. Only by being concise, compelling and value driven have I been able to achieve any of these results.

SUMMARY

As with most anything, what matters most is not how much information you have to convey to your network, it is the quality. Whether communicating in the real world or through LinkedIn, make your message concise, compelling and value-driven.

LinkedWorking

DARE TO ASK

"Teamwork is the ability to work together toward a common vision. The ability to direct individual accomplishments toward organizational objectives. It is the fuel that allows common people to attain uncommon results."

Andrew Carnegie

REAL WORLD NETWORKING LESSON

You have achieved nothing alone. Every step of the way, whether you are willing to admit it or not, someone provided assistance. Perhaps a friend made an introduction that led you to a new client. Or a client sent you an article that gave you that wonderful, money-saving idea. Perhaps a colleague has a brother-in-law at a major publication that just happens to be looking for your unique story.

We do nothing alone. Our networks are the source of all of our accomplishments, achievements and milestones. Knowing this, how can we tap into our networks to obtain more or accelerate these successes? Simple: Just ask.

Years ago, my father shared an insight. He called it the "Pretty Girl" Syndrome. He asserted that some times the attractive girls do not go to prom or other formal social functions because no one asks them. The reason no one asks is that everyone assumes that the "pretty girl" already has a date - and she is too proud to lead on otherwise.

This insight has applications relative to achieving success and networking, which is actually the context in which my father shared it with me. When you are successful or well networked, few people look to help you.

The reality, however, is that you have a degree of success and you have a reasonably well-established network. As a result, if you want to get assistance from your network, you need to ask. In fact, unless you ask for things, you will get nothing.

Ask your network for anything that can help you. Ask for those key contacts that lead to new clients, vendors or employees. Ask for information related to your competition or industry. Ask for advice or ideas to advance your career, business or personal life.

If you are reluctant to access your network in this manner because you feel that asking seems too much like a cry for help or an admission of weakness, you need to change your mindset. Approaching your network for assistance is a declaration of your desire to succeed.

If you are hesitant to tap into your network because this might be an imposition on your friends, relations or business colleagues, change your way of thinking. The truth is that your network is both interested and eager to help you. Your network does not fail you. Rather, you fail - fail to make friends, relations or business colleagues aware of how they can assist you.

Next time you are reluctant to access your network, whether to review a resumé, to meet a new client, locate industry information or whatever, remember this: If you do not ask, chances are nothing will happen. If, however, you ask for assistance, life guarantees you a chance.

In asking, however, you need to adhere to three basic rules of networking to make your requests most effective. First, you need to be of a giving nature first. People will help if you ask and if they know, like and trust you. To ensure that others like you, you need to demonstrate a willingness to help them first. If you embrace many of the earlier chapters of this book, you will be doing this.

Second, remember that asking from others does not suggest that you have a license to sell. In other words, you are not asking someone to buy your insurance, invest with you or be your client. You are asking them for information, assistance and maybe introductions.

If asking another is an attempt to sell (even a veiled attempt to sell), not only will you fail to make a sale, but you will also taint yourself with respect to that particular person.

Finally, when you ask of others, remember to be specific. While others want to give you assistance, they need guidance in determining how to assist you. After all, you do not go through the McDonald's Drive-Thru and say, "Give me some food." You are specific - "I would like a Big Mac, large fries and a small shake."

The same is true of networking. You will be more successful asking somewhat explicit questions. For example:

- **RATHER THAN:** Do you have any business contacts?

  USE: Do you know anyone that works for Banner Stamping or any other small manufacturer in the area?

- **RATHER THAN:** Can you help me get my business networked?

  USE: Can you get me information on the networking events you have found beneficial?

- **RATHER THAN:** Would you help me with my career?

  USE: Would you review my resumé and help me work through some mock interview questions?

In summary, following my father's metaphor, you need to resolve not to become that beautiful woman home alone on the night of the ball.

If you add value to your network (whether in the form of giving referrals, making introductions or supplying information), there is nothing wrong with looking to get some value in return. To do so, however, you need to ask for what you want.

APPLYING THE LESSON TO LINKEDIN

What is the purpose of building a network on LinkedIn if you never use it? You build this network for a reason: So you can use the resources to help you become more successful.

When you reach out to a potential connection, in a humble, yet informative way, they will want to help you. In a post from *The Blog Of Tim Ferriss* (go to http://www.fourhourworkweek.com/blog and search "5 Tips For E-mailing Busy People"), the author gives some guidelines for e-mailing anyone, some of which include:

1. Be brief and make sure what you are requesting is clear. No "let's jump on the phone for 10 minutes; it'll be worth your time."

2. Do not send "keeping in touch" e-mails, as this only further over-burdens those you are contacting.

3. Explicitly state what you have done to get answers or help yourself. Make it clear that you are doing your part, and have explored other avenues before asking for someone's help. It is amazing how many people ask busier people for answers Google could provide in seconds.

4. Make it clear that it is all right if they cannot help or if they are too committed elsewhere. This, paradoxically, makes it much more likely to get a response.

These tenets should be used for every e-mail request to anyone. Remember, e-mail is like food. Good recipes produce good results, but only if you follow the proper steps.

One of the biggest reasons I have had success in connecting with top industry leaders and online celebrities is because I took action by contacting and asking. You have nothing to lose when contacting someone on LinkedIn.

You do not have to worry about stumbling over your words, looking nervous or making a fool out of yourself, because you control what you draft in the e-mail, being shy should never hold anyone back. Besides, if you make a brief introduction, and provide a value to the person you are connecting with, more times than not they will at least reply.

Once you connect with these interesting individuals you need to take it to the next level and Ask. What should you ask for? Normally there are four main things people ask for on LinkedIn:

1. **Recommendations:** You can ask for a personal recommendation for your profile, or ask for a recommendation of a job opportunity of which someone may be aware.

2. **Answers:** Ask for answers or advice pertaining to a question only that person can answer. Do not ask them a question that a simple Google search could find 1,358,007 answers for in 0.09 seconds.

3. **Introductions:** Ask graciously for introductions that will add value to your network.

4. **Face-To-Face-Meetings:** Ask to meet up if you are in a central location. Although LinkedIn is a great tool for building your network, it does not replace being face-to-face and building a real personal relationship.

Ask them if they would be open to a brief phone conversation once you have established credibility and have something worthwhile to discuss. Ask industry leaders if they will be attending the next trade show or conference, and if they would be willing to meet for a brief introduction. Build some rapport and credibility, then Ask, Ask, Ask! This is the only way you will get anything from your network.

SUCCESS STORY

Sheilah Etheridge, Owner and Consultant, SME Management
LinkedIn: www.LinkedIn.com/in/smemanagement

Sheilah Etheridge is an Accounting and Business Management specialist based in Anchorage, Alaska. On a contract basis, she provides a wide range of services including bookkeeping, full accounting, payroll, business and personal management, audits and audit preparation.

Sheilah is known as the "Queen of Q&A" on LinkedIn. At the release of this book she had over 730 best answers on the topic of using LinkedIn, approximately 30 best answers on Professional Networking, 28 on Staffing and Recruiting, 20 in Accounting, and hundreds more in 91 other question categories with LinkedIn. Not only is she the queen of answering questions, she has also asked hundreds of questions, and usually gets over 50 answers on a majority of her thought-provoking topics.

HER STORY ... HER WORDS

LinkedIn can work for you just as it has worked for me and millions of other people who have been willing to invest the time and energy necessary to reap the rewards. And, yes ... it all begins when you dare to ask.

Everything about networking is a two-way street. Ask a question and start the process of mingling with the crowd. Or answer someone else's question. The key is to just be yourself and share your knowledge with others, or gain from their knowledge. Just remember it is also important to thank those that have answered your questions.

If you want to get introduced to someone don't be shy. Ask for an introduction to them through a shared connection. Be direct and be sincere, and let the person know why you are reaching out to them to connect. It does not have to be because you want to do business, it may be you were simply impressed with something you read about them and want to get to know them better. However, don't use InMails and introductions for cold calling. That is a huge mistake people make, and it is always the quickest way to lose out on doing business with that person down the road.

Whether you are networking live and in person or on LinkedIn, it all comes down to the same thing. You must be willing to open yourself up to the possibilities.

I have had great success with networking because I get to know the people in my network. We e-mail, chat and talk on the phone. We all pay it forward. If you get to know the person behind the title or the company first, you will be amazed at all the possibilities that present themselves.

Many people make the mistake of focusing solely on the business side. However, by allowing others to get to know who you are as a person, and you getting to know who they are, you will often find commonalities that pave the way to doing business together. It is all a part of building trust within your network.

This can be accomplished in many ways. I believe that the Answers section of LinkedIn is the best place to begin. Whether you are asking a question or answering one, you have the opportunity to get to know the mindset of the members and find people with which to network.

Joining groups is another method that allows a great deal of insight into one another, how each person thinks, and how they approach business and problem solving. That, coupled with e-mails and chats, allows you to develop a truer sense of who these people are. In the end, you will know the LinkedIn members better than you do many of the people you network with in real life.

The rewards come in many ways. I have gained clients from my time on LinkedIn, for both short- and long-term projects. In fact, one of my clients came as a result of my helping a gentleman back East who had asked a question on LinkedIn. I answered his question, and the dialog continued. Before I knew it, he had more questions.

We connected and I offered help where I could. In the process we got to know each other and he was quite comfortable with my level of knowledge in my field. Time passed and one day the telephone rang. It was a lady here in Anchorage who was looking for a new consultant and accountant. We spoke for a few minutes and then she told me she had gotten my name from a friend of hers in New York, who happened to be the guy I had helped. It really is a small world. It never occurred to me he would know anyone in Alaska, much less send a new client my way. That is just one example. I have also done countless short-term projects for people I have met through LinkedIn.

Many of us do business around the world, and often we find we need a little cultural insight before traveling overseas or making a conference call. Cultural differences can make or break a business deal. On LinkedIn we can reach out and get all the help we need from business people in any country in the world, and all we need to do is ... dare to ask.

Due to my participation in the Answers section (both asking and answering questions), I have become rather well known and as a result I have had job offers when I wasn't even looking for a job. It is amazing how many opportunities can drop in your lap without you even asking.

As a result of my asking questions (and answering them), and taking the time to get to know my network, I was fortunate enough to be one of the first interviews Stan Relihan did when he started his Podcast. Interestingly, over a year later I am still getting e-mails from people who have listened to the podcast and want to connect or brainstorm.

I have done several other interviews as well, such as Money magazine, and with numerous bloggers. More amazingly, Stan and another podcaster who had interviewed Vint Cerf (co-founder of the internet) had a contest to see which podcast (mine or Vint Cerf's) got the most "diggs." I am proud to say, but not surprised, that mine won.

I have been invited to be a speaker at almost every LinkedIn live network that exists. Time is tight and I have not had the opportunity to go speak at any of these events (other than local ones), but the invitation is there and waiting for me anytime.

There is hardly a place in the world I could travel to and not know someone with whom I could share a meal with or see while I am there. How many times in the past have you been stuck in a strange city and not known a soul? That will not happen again....if you dare to ask. I was also named as a VIP guest for a LinkedIn live cruise, and was invited to attend, all expenses paid.

I have also had the great pleasure of being instrumental in helping a large number of people get jobs, meet the right recruiter or start their own business.

Much of this is, of course, while not a gain in a monetary nature, is a true investment in human life. LinkedIn is all about paying it forward, and I believe our investment of time and energy is always rewarded.

I think the people are the greatest reward for me. In many ways LinkedIn has renewed my faith in mankind. That may sound silly to you, but I assure you it isn't. In a day and age where many are only in it for themselves, this site allows us to see that good and caring people with bright minds and a desire to help others as well as themselves still exist. Just look at the incredible wealth of knowledge that is FREELY shared in the

Answers section all day, every day. You don't see that in real life. In real life there is always a price tag attached, but not on LinkedIn.

I have given and received a wealth of knowledge on this site and I am constantly learning and teaching new things and new thought processes. You can't beat that. And it is all there for the taking ... if you dare to ask.

SUMMARY

It does not matter who you are...what type of business you own...or what company you work for, you can enhance your network if you commit to establishing great relationships, giving to them freely and then ask for assistance when you need it.

PERSIST PATIENTLY

*"Most of the important things in the world have been
accomplished by people who have kept on trying when there
seemed to be no hope at all."*
Dale Carnegie

REAL WORLD NETWORKING LESSON

Networking is about building life-long contacts that you
can draw upon and contribute to for assistance. Building
this sort of network is largely a function of creating solid
relationships. And creating solid relationships, by its very
nature, takes time and cannot be rushed.

It takes time to find the right people. It takes time to
develop the mutual knowing, liking and trusting of one
another. It takes time to understand how the value you have
serves to benefit the needs of others (and vice versa). Far too
often, some will embark upon networking as if it is simply
a function of quickly organizing a collection of people for
some limited purpose, such as finding a job. Shortly after this
campaign begins, their efforts do not produce the results they
want and they then declare that "networking doesn't work."

Networking does work, however. It has always worked,
if done properly. A couple hundred-thousand years ago,
humans appeared on earth and ventured forth. Then in a
mere tick of the geological clock, we literally populated every
nook and cranny of the globe. How did this occur? Simple.
Humans developed ways of interacting and ensuring one
another's success. In short, humans discovered that they not
only improved their chances of survival, but also increased
their level of prosperity by simply sharing labor, tools and
information. This was early networking.

It did not stop there, however. It has guided us through history. It has been a part of your entire life. You networked as a child, swapping cookies for potato chips at lunch. You networked as a teen, which is how you got the Senior English notes for the day you were absent. And you continue to network as an adult, which is probably how you came to hear about this book.

Networking is a part of life and it works. It is important to note, however, that there is no time requirement associated with building a network. If fact, you should and will always be building it. While there is no time requirement, you should endeavor that it be built to be strong and productive, no matter how long that takes you. So it is essential that you employ patience and persistence in the process.

Consider President Garfield's response to impatience when he served as the President of Hiram College: "When God wants to make an oak tree, he takes 100 years. When he wants to make a squash, he requires only two months."

As you work to grow and develop your network, what is your mindset? Are you seeking to build a mighty oak tree, or simply a puny pumpkin?

APPLYING THE LESSON TO LINKEDIN

It takes time to build your LinkedIn network. It is important to persist patiently and not be concerned with what others are doing.

Your mission on LinkedIn is to follow the ABB's of networking: Always Be Building your network. Whether you are trying to find a job, create new opportunities, close more deals, make more money or become a globally recognized industry leader, the success factor for every networker is to Always Be Building your network of connections and opportunities.

Here are some simple suggestions to help fulfill the ABB's of networking on LinkedIn daily:

- **Add New Contacts:** As LinkedIn continues to grow at a few million members per month, more of your "real world" contacts will begin to join. Periodically, go to the "Add Connections" tab on your LinkedIn home page and see who has recently joined from your e-mail address book. Send them all invites to link up.

- **Invite Friends:** Occasionally, seek out friends or colleagues who are not currently on LinkedIn who could benefit from it. Send them a personal invite to join, and briefly explain to them the benefits of building their network online.

- **Optimize Your Profile:** Every so often, update your LinkedIn profile with rich key words and phrases to bring your profile to the top of the list when others search for those specific words. The more others find you from the search box, the more likely they will reach out to connect.

- **Ask Questions:** Once in a while, ask a compelling question-one where you are bound to get a few responses. Remember each group has a discussion platform that allows you to become more involved with members. Then start to connect with those members.

- **Answer Questions:** Whenever you get the chance, add value to the questions others ask by providing insightful answers. Others will appreciate this and will seek to connect with you on other topics in the future.

- **Recommend Others:** Whenever appropriate, make a recommendation for someone. When you recommend others, your name and recommendation show up on their profile. The more profiles you recommend, the more times your name shows up when others browse those profiles. Eventually, they will start to add you to their network if they like what they read.

How will you know if you have made progress over a period of time? You do this by benchmarking your results. A good way to benchmark your progress on LinkedIn is to start off by writing down the:

- Number of connections you have
- Number of recommendations you have written
- Number of recommendations you have received
- Number of questions you have asked
- Number of questions you have answered
- Number of groups you are in
- Number of members in any groups you have created
- Number of business leads you have received
- Number of phone conversations with new connections
- Number of face-to-face meetings with new connections

Once you write down what you already have for each category, place this in an envelope and seal it for six months. At the end of the six months, check back to your numbers in the envelope. This way you can see where you started, and look at how far you have come. You should notice a huge difference in every aspect of your LinkedIn experience.

SUCCESS STORY

Kelly Perdew, CEO, Rotohog.com and
Winner of *The Apprentice 2*

LinkedIn: www.LinkedIn.com/in/kellyperdew
Website: www.kellyperdew.com & www.rotohog.com

Kelly Perdew is an entrepreneur at heart. While he is best known for winning Season 2 of Donald Trump's *The Apprentice*, he really loves the challenge of starting and growing businesses. He has served in every capacity ... founder ... board member ... CEO ... financing ... growing businesses ... down-sizing businesses ... and selling businesses for eight figures. It was his connections and activity on LinkedIn that got him the position as CEO of Rotohog.com, a software provider and operator of fantasy sports products and platforms.

HIS STORY ... HIS WORDS

I initially got on LinkedIn at the beginning of its existence, and instantly saw the value in using it. Because of the value I witnessed, I became a power user right out of the gate. During this time, *The Apprentice* had become a hit TV show after its first season. My family and friends told me that this show was designed specifically for my personality so I decided to try out. Getting on *The Apprentice* was a challenging process, and Donald Trump says there are over one million people who apply each year, so making it on was an accomplishment in itself.

I contacted the head of business development at LinkedIn when I was on episode 12 of the 16 episodes showing on NBC. I told them who I was, and that I was a finalist on the show. I proposed that I would write about LinkedIn in my book, feature them on my website and talk about them at every event at which I spoke. I did not know if I would win, but when it happened I was able to negotiate some stock in LinkedIn. LinkedIn had my picture on their home page, announcing that one of their members won the show, and I actually became the "face" of the site for about two weeks.

My main success coming from LinkedIn was that someone found me online, and I was recruited to be the CEO of Rotohog.com. I had answered someone's question online and ended up inviting that person to a networking event. The person I invited said that they were looking for a person to fill the CEO role for Rotohog, and thought I would be the right person for the job.

Yes, I have had great success both through and from LinkedIn. And looking back at all the success, you might say to yourself, "This guy had it easy" or "He just lucked out." While admittedly I had some opportunities, and I did make some right decisions at the appropriate times, there were still major elements of persistence and patience to all that I have achieved on LinkedIn.

All the success did not happen instantly. There was effort. I invited people to link with me, and I invited people to connect with me in the real world. I posed questions and I answered questions. I re-worked and tinkered with my profile. None of this happened overnight. I just had to keep after it.

Networking is critical to success. You have to be actively networking all the time. Whether you feel comfortable in your job, or are worried about finding a new job, it is imperative to be persistent and use all of the networking tools at your disposal, at all times - especially LinkedIn. The more you work on building your network, the more this will give you the advantage to reach out to those you know when the times get tough. There is no question that LinkedIn is a great way to patiently persist and actively build your network.

SUMMARY

Networking works, in the real world and on LinkedIn. However, that does not always mean that it works as quickly as you might like. Nevertheless, it works. Therefore, your best course of action is to keep after it.

LINKEDWORKING IN SUMMARY

LinkedIn does work! Or at least, LinkedIn can work if you use it properly. The evidence is there. Today, there are literally thousands (perhaps even tens of thousands) of people who are making new productive contacts, finding great opportunities and generally experiencing success on LinkedIn.

The question is: "Does what Lewis suggests work?" I had no doubt before we started that Lewis was generating success on LinkedIn - I believed every word he said. As we wrote, he continued to realize success from working with LinkedIn - I watched as he jetted from here to there. And I am confident that he will continue to find success working with LinkedIn - he has developed an almost unstoppable wave of momentum on LinkedIn.

What I pondered as we started to write the initial draft of this book was whether or not there was really merit in the notion of LinkedWorking. Yes, Lewis experienced success. The issue was, however, whether his success was unique to him or whether his methods were something that others would succeed by undertaking. After all, while I felt confident Lewis was simply applying plain old networking activities on LinkedIn, I did not know enough about LinkedIn to be completely confident in my conclusions.

So I did what any curious person would do. I put Lewis' actions to the test. When we first met to talk about his success on LinkedIn, I took lots of notes. Long before Lewis laid out his activities in this book, he had provided me with a formula - one that I could follow and see for myself.

As we began to outline LinkedWorking, I began working behind the scenes to implement the very content of the book. While in totality this could be considered a massive undertaking, it did not seem like it.

Following what Lewis recommended, I simply did a little each day and was patient regarding the results.

First, I took the time to re-work my profile, really thinking through the message I wanted to convey. Then, I contacted those in my "real world" network that I knew were or thought could be on LinkedIn, to invite them to connect with me. Additionally, I freely accepted invitations from those wanting to connect with me.

Using the search feature, I found and joined a variety of groups that were aligned with my interests. Once accepted into these groups, I did not passively sit back. Rather, I began immersing myself in these groups - looking for people with whom to connect, engaging in discussions and even starting discussions. Furthermore, in areas where I could not find a group to join, I created one and then set about trying to find people to join.

As we worked through the drafting of the book, I found myself adding LinkedIn activities to what I was doing. By the time we started the editing, I had a complete regimen of new functions to periodically deploy on LinkedIn.

When this process started, I had a presence on LinkedIn and that was about it. I did have a respectable number of connections at the time (or so I was told). In my mind, this was to be expected just by the sheer volume of contacts I have through AmSpirit Business Connections and my other involvements. Compared to my "real world" network, however, my LinkedIn network was puny.

When this process started, not surprisingly, being on LinkedIn was doing very little for me. Yes, I did happen to reconnect with some old friends and colleagues. There was little beyond that. However, once I started to implement the ideas that Lewis had written about, essentially taking my own networking medicine on LinkedIn, things began to happen for me. I found that I was getting more and more opportunities to talk with people about AmSpirit Business Connections, not just in Columbus, Ohio, but around the United States.

Before I started this process, in franchising AmSpirit Business Connections, I only had one or two people at a time in my potential franchisee pipeline. Fast forward to today, and that number has increased ten fold and continues to grow.

For the last several years, I have produced an event in Columbus referred to as CONES - Central Ohio Networking Event and Social. Before we started writing this book, the event had a record number of sponsors - 46. After we started writing and I began LinkedWorking, the event had 109 total sponsors.

Beyond professional development books (this and *Foundational Networking*), I have written two novels (*Out of the Comfort Zone* and *Rival*). Prior to really embracing LinkedIn as Lewis advocates, sales from these works of fiction depended upon close friends and family. After practicing LinkedWorking, I find that I sell books to people I do not know and people I will likely never meet, from every corner of the United States.

Yes, LinkedWorking works. From my experience, that is what I have concluded. It takes some work, as there is no magic here. Nevertheless, if you are willing to consistently put in some effort on LinkedIn and follow what we have set forth in this book, you will conclude the same, and you will generate opportunities, contacts and success in the process.

ARE YOU LOOKING FOR MORE?

Are you interested in being further empowered and inspired by *LinkedWorking* or networking in general, then visit ...

www.linkedworking.com

www.amspirit.com

www.sportsnetworker.com

A LITTLE ABOUT FRANK AGIN

Frank Agin is the founder and president of AmSpirit Business Connections, where he works to empower entrepreneurs, sales representatives and professionals around the country to become more successful through networking.

In addition to co-authoring *LinkedWorking: Generating Success on the World's Largest Professional Networking Website*, he is the author of *Foundational Networking: Building Know, Like and Trust to Create a Lifetime of Extraordinary Success*.

Along with these books, he has also written numerous articles on professional networking, continues to collaborate with respect to various e-books and is a monthly contributor to SportsNetworker. com, an online newsletter and blog where he writes a sports-themed networking advice column, The Huddle.

Frank is also a sought after speaker and consultant to companies and organizations on topics related to professional networking and business relationship development.

Frank has a law degree and MBA from the Ohio State University and a BA in economics and management from Beloit College.

He lives with his wife in Blacklick, Ohio. When he is not working, he enjoys home improvement projects, working out and watching his three children participate in sports. As for community involvement, he is active with the St. Matthew Athletic Association and the Houghton High School Alumni Association. He is also an avid fiction writer, with two novels to his credit: *Out of the Comfort Zone* and *RIVAL*.

You can find more information about Frank Agin either at www.frankagin.com or on his LinkedIn profile. You can contact him directly at frankagin@amspirit.com.

A LITTLE ABOUT LEWIS HOWES

Lewis Howes is the founder of SportsNetworker.com, a publication that provides insider opinions, interviews and resources to help professional athletes and sports executives advance their careers in the sports industry.

Along with being the co-author of *LinkedWorking: Generating Success on the World's Largest Professional Networking Website*, he consults with business professionals and companies on how to more effectively use LinkedIn to attract new business. He also hosts a series of live LinkedIn networking events around the country, conducts LinkedIn training seminars, and speaks on social media networking and other related topics.

In addition, Lewis is also an inventor and intellectual property broker with Trident Design, LLC (www.trident-design.com), a high-powered innovation firm based in Columbus, Ohio.

Lewis has a Sports Management degree with a focus on business from Principia College, where he set the NCAA record for receiving yards in a single game (418 yards) and was a two-sport All-American in football and track.

After a successful couple years playing professional football, he moved to Columbus, Ohio. When he is not working, he enjoys salsa dancing, playing the guitar with his gifted family of musicians and staying in shape. He is involved with Toastmasters International and still has a passion for playing sports, which is why he competes in everything he undertakes.

You can find more information about Lewis Howes either at www.lewishowes.com or on his LinkedIn profile. You can contact him directly at lewis@lewishowes.com.

Frank Agin & Lewis Howes

LinkedWorking

Breinigsville, PA USA
24 June 2010
240543BV00001B/125/P

9 780982 333204